Charles M. Clement

Charter and Ordinances of the Borough of Sunbury

with the provisions of the Constitution and general laws of the State relating to

boroughs, and the by-laws and rules of order of the Town Council

Charles M. Clement

Charter and Ordinances of the Borough of Sunbury
with the provisions of the Constitution and general laws of the State relating to boroughs,
and the by-laws and rules of order of the Town Council

ISBN/EAN: 9783337301989

Printed in Europe, USA, Canada, Australia, Japan

Cover: Foto ©Suzi / pixelio.de

More available books at **www.hansebooks.com**

CHARTER AND ORDINANCES

OF THE

BOROUGH OF SUNBURY,

WITH THE

PROVISIONS OF THE CONSTITUTION AND GENERAL LAWS OF THE STATE RELATING TO BOROUGHS, AND THE BY-LAWS AND RULES OF ORDER OF THE TOWN COUNCIL.

COMPILED BY DIRECTION

OF THE

BOROUGH COUNCIL

BY

CHARLES M. CLEMENT.

EICHHOLTZ & CO., PRINTERS, SUNBURY, PA.
1886.

PREFACE.

The laws are arranged chronologically, the full text being given in each instance. This is done for the double purpose of presenting a historical view of the legislation for the borough and to enable the reader to ascertain, with the least difficulty, just what laws were in force at any date. Where the provisions of any law have been modified by subsequent enactment, or have been supplied by a general law, these facts are set out in foot notes. The provisions of the Constitution of 1873, relative to boroughs and all general laws relating to municipal government enacted since then have been inserted, so as to make this book a digest of "Sunbury borough law."

In compiling the ordinances, the book published in 1855 and the written ordinance book of the council have been used as guides, as far as possible, verifying them by the minute books; and the compiler would acknowledge the assistance he has received in this part of his work from the very efficient town clerk, Mr. Lewis D. Haupt.

CHARTER.

An ACT to erect the town of Sunbury, in the County of Northumberland, into a borough.

SECTION I. *Be it enacted by the Senate and House of Representatives of the commonwealth of Pennsylvania, in General Assembly met, and it is hereby enacted by the authority of the same,* That the town of Sunbury shall be, and the same is hereby, erected into a borough, which shall be called "The Borough of Sunbury," forever; the extent of which said borough is and shall be comprised within the following boundaries, to wit; beginning at the mouth of Shamokin creek, where it empties into the river Susquehanna, at low water-mark; thence up the said creek, on the north side thereof, to the mouth of the gut; thence up the same, on the west side thereof, to the line of Samuel Scott's land, and by the same to the river aforsaid, at low water-mark; thence down the same river, at low water-mark, to the place of beginning.

a. 5 Bioren 232, The town of Sunbury erected into a borough. Its boundaries.

Its boundaries.

SEC. II. *And be it further enacted by the authority aforesaid,* That it shall and may be lawful for such of the inhabitants as are entitled to vote for Members of the Legislature, and who have resided within the said borough for at least one whole year next preceding any such elections as are hereinafter directed, on the first Monday in May, in the year of our Lord one thousand seven hundred and ninety-seven, and on that day yearly thereafter forever, publicly to meet at the

b. 5 Bioren 233. Certain officers of the borough, when to be elected.

a. What is known as "Caketown" was annexed to the borough by Act of 19th April, 1853, P. L., Page 589; then re-annexed to the township by Act of 2d April, 1860, P. L. 522, and again attached to the borough by the Act of 2d April, 1867, P. L. 657.

b. All borough elections are now held on the third Tuesday in February, as fixed by the Constitution of 1873, and are regulated by the general election laws; sixty days residence is therefore sufficient.

Court House in said borough, until a market house shall be erected therein, and from and after erecting a market house, then at the same, and then and there to nominate, elect and choose, by ballot, two of the inhabitants of the said borough to be Burgesses, one to be High Constable, and one to be Town Clerk, and four inhabitants as aforesaid to be Assistants within the same, for assisting the said Burgesses in managing the affairs of the borough, and in keeping the peace and good order therein; which election shall be held from time to time by the High Constable of the year preceding; and the names of the persons so elected shall be certified under his seal, to the Governor of the Commonwealth for the time being, within thirty days next after such election; and the Burgess who shall have the majority of votes shall be called the Chief Burgess of the said borough; but if the votes shall be equal, the Governor shall determine which shall be Chief Burgess. And in case it should so happen that the said inhabitants shall neglect or refuse to choose Burgesses, and the said other officers, in manner aforesaid, that then it shall and may be lawful for the Governor to nominate, appoint and commissionate Burgesses, High Constable, Town Clerk and Assistants, for that year, to hold and continue in their respective offices until the next time of annual election appointed as aforesaid, and so often as occasion shall require.

By Act of 16th March, 1803, (7 Bioren Page 34.) The election of eight common councilmen was authorized, who with the Burgesses and Assisstants should make the "common council."

By Act of 19th February, 1863, one person was to be elected as Chief Burgess and one person as Second Burgess.

By Act of 17th March, 1865, the council are authorized to appoint a town clerk and high constable, whenever these offices become vacant.

Under the Act dividing the borough into East and West wards, two of the Assistants were elected in each of the wards. When the borough was divided into five wards, under the provisions of the Act of 1874 and its supplements, the title of the Second Burgess was changed to "Assistant Burgess," and the four Assistants as provided for in this section ceased to exist.

Sec. III. *And be it further enacted by the authority aforesaid,* That the said Burgesses and inhabitants within the said borough, and their successors, for ever hereafter, shall be one body corporate and politic, in deed and name, and by the name of "The Burgesses and inhabitants of the borough of Sunbury, in the County of Northumberland," shall have a perpetual succession; and they, and their successors, by the name of "The Burgesses and inhabitants of the Borough of "Sunbury," shall at all times hereafter be persons able and capable in law to have, get, receive and possess lands, tenements and hereditaments, to them and their successors, in fee-simple, or for term of life, lives, years or otherwise, and also rents, goods and chattels, and other things, of what nature or kind soever, and also to give, grant, let, sell and assign the same lands, tenements, rents, goods and chattels and to do and execute all other things about the same by the name aforesaid; and they shall forever hereafter be persons able and capable in law to sue and be sued, plead and be impleaded, answer and be answered unto, defend and be defended, in all or any of the courts, within this Commonwealth, in all manner of actions, suits, complaints, pleas, causes, and matters whatsoever; and that it shall and may be lawful to and for the said Burgesses and inhabitants of the Borough of Sunbury aforesaid, and their successors forever hereafter, to have and use one common seal, for sealing of all business whatsoever touching the said Corporation, and the same from time to time, at their will, to change and alter.

The Burgesses and freeholders made a body corporate, with powers of acquiring and holding real and personal estate, &c.

Sec. IV. *And be it further enacted by the authority aforesaid,* That it shall and may be lawful for the Burgesses and inhabitants of the said borough, and their successors, to have, hold and keep, at the place appropriated, or to be appropri-

5 Bioren 234. c. Markets, when to be held.

---

c. By the Act of 3d April, 1872, P. L. Page 860, the council was authorized to make all needful regulations respecting markets and market days. The council has by ordinance, fixed Tuesday, Thursday and Saturday as market days.

ated, for a market house within the said borough, two markets in each week, that is to say ; one market on Wednesday and one market on Saturday, in every week of the year, forever, together with free liberties, customs, profits and emoluments, to the said market belonging, or in any wise appertaining, forever ; and there shall be a Clerk of the market within the said borough, who shall and may perform all things belonging to the office of a Clerk of the market within the said borough, and shall be removeable by the Burgesses and Assistants aforesaid, and another from time to time appointed and removed, as they shall find necessary.

Clerk of the
market to be
appointed.

SEC. V. *And be it further enacted by the authority aforesaid,* That the Burgesses and inhabitants of the Borough of Sunbury may and shall, at their own cost and charge, make or cause to be made a sufficient causeway over and across the wide public way lying along the bank of the Susquehanna, and extending to low water mark, as may be most convenient, and make or cause to be made a sufficient landing-place at the side of the said river, on such causeway, and shall at all times hereafter keep and maintain the same in good repair, fit for men, horses and carriages, to pass and repass ; and also provide a good substantial ferry-boat or boats, and capable ferry-men, who shall reside and dwell in the said Borough of Sunbury, and duly and constantly attend the same, as occasion may require.

The Corpora-
tion may make
a causeway a-
cross the pub-
lic way along
the Susquehan-
na, and a land-
ing place; and
provide ferry-
boats.

SEC. VI. And for the better encouragement of the said ferry, *Be it further enacted by the authority aforesaid,* 'that no person or persons whatsoever shall keep or use any boat or canoe, for transporting any person or persons, horses or cattle, carriages or commodities, for hire or pay, over the said river, from the Borough of Sunbury, besides the ferry hereby established, under the penalty of fifty dollars, current money of this Commonwealth, to be recovered in any court

d. No other
person shall
keep a ferry at
that place.

---

d. The right of ferriage has been conferred on the Sunbury Steam Ferry and Tow Boat Company by the Act of 5th April, 1870, P. L. 871, but this section is not repealed and the borough's right still exists.

of record of this Commonwealth, one half thereof to the use
of the informer or prosecutor, who shall sue for the same,
and the other half to the use of the Burgesses and inhabitants of the said borough, wherein no more than one imparlance shall be allowed; which said ferry shall be subject to
such rules, rates and regulations, as the Court of Quarter
Sessions of the County of Northumberland in future may
direct and appoint.

SEC. VII. *And be it further enacted by the authority aforesaid,*
That the Burgesses and inhabitants of the Borough of Sunbury, respectively, forever, shall enjoy all the powers, juris-
dictions, authorities and privileges, and be subject to the
same qualifications, restrictions, penalties, fines and forfeitures, within the said borough, as are enjoyed by and limited
to the Burgesses and inhabitants of the Borough of Reading in the County of Berks, excepting only the liberty of holding fairs, the powers vested in the inhabitants of Reading
by the twenty-ninth fection of the act incorporating that
borough, and so much of the said act, as is altered and supplied by this act.

Passed 24th March, 1797.

e. 5 Bioren 235.
Powers and
privileges of
the borough of
Sunbury.

THAT PART OF THE ACT OF INCORPORATION OF THE BOR-
OUGH OF READING, WHICH APPLIES TO THE
BOROUGH OF SUNBURY.

SEC. VIII. *And be it further enacted by the authority afore-*
said, That before any of the said Burgesses, Constable, Town
Clerk, or other officers, shall take upon themselves their respective offices, they shall take and subscribe such oath or
affirmation of allegiance and fidelity, as by the laws of the
Commonwealth are in such cases provided, together with the
oath or affirmation for the due execution of their respective

a. 2 Bioren 421.
Qualifications
of officers.

---

e. By Act of 22d January, 1802, (6 Bioren 214,) yearly fairs were authorized
in Sunbury, with all the privileges &c., incident to fairs in Reading.

a. The terms of office of all borough officers by general law, commence on
the first Monday in March following their election.

offices; and every Chief Burgess, so elected or appointed from year to year, as aforesaid, shall, within ten days immediately after his election, take the oath or affirmation aforesaid, before a Justice of the Peace for the county aforesaid; and that on his failure to take the oath or affirmation aforesaid, within the time aforesaid (unless disabled by sickness, or other reasonable cause) another Chief Burgess shall, from time to time, and as often as occasion shall require, be appointed by the President in Council, in the stead of such person so failing to appear and qualify himself as aforesaid; which Burgess, so to be appointed by the President and Council, shall and may hold and enjoy his office until the day of election next ensuing the day of his appointment; and the Chief Burgess, having qualified himself in manner aforesaid, shall enter upon his office; and the other Burgess, Constable, Town Clerk, or other officers, shall and may qualify themselves for their respective offices, by taking and subscribing the oaths or affirmations aforesaid before the said Chief Burgess, or before one of the Justices of the Peace of the said county, who are hereby authorized and empowered to administer the same.

SEC. IX. *And be it further enacted by the authority aforesaid,* That it shall and may be lawful for the Burgesses, freeholders and inhabitants, housekeepers, aforesaid, and their successors, to have, hold and keep, within the said borough, two markets in each week; that is to say, one market on Wednesday, and one on Saturday, in every week of the year, forever, in the center square of the said borough; and two fairs in the year, the first to begin on the fourth day of June, one thousand seven hundred and eighty-four, and the other of said fairs to begin on the twenty-seventh day of October following, each fair to continue two days; and when either of those days shall happen to fall on Sunday, then the said fairs to be kept the next day or two days following; togeth-

b. 2 Bioren 422.
Markets and
fairs.

---

b. This section is now obsolete. See note on Sec. IV of Sunbury charter.

er with free liberties, customs, profits and emoluments, to the said markets and fairs belonging, and in any wise appertaining, forever; And that there shall be a clerk of the market of the said borough, who shall have the affize of bread, wine, beer, wood, and all other provisions, brought for the use of the inhabitants, and who shall and may perform all things belonging to the office of a clerk of the market within the said borough.

Clerk of the market.

SEC. X. *And be it further enacted by the authority aforesaid,* That if any of the inhabitants of the said borough shall hereafter be elected to the office of Burgesses, High Constable or Assistants, and, having notice of his or their election, shall refuse to undertake and execute that office to which he is chosen, it shall and may be lawful for the Burgesses, High Constable and Assistants, then acting, to impose such moderate fines on the person or persons so refusing, as to them shall seem meet; so always, that a fine imposed on a Burgess elect do not exceed the sum of ten pounds, and the fine of a High Constable or Assistant elect do not exceed the sum of five pounds each; to be levied by distress and sale of the goods of the party refusing, by warrant under the hand and seal of one of the said Burgesses, or by any other lawful ways or means whatsoever, for the use of the said corporation; and in any such case, it shall and may be lawful for the said inhabitants to proceed to the choice of some other fit person or persons, in the stead of such who shall so refuse.

Pena'ty on officers elect refusing or neglecting to act.

SEC. XI. *And be it further enacted by the authority aforesaid,* That it shall and may be lawful for the said Burgesses, High Constable and Assistants, for the time being, to assemble town-meetings, as often as they shall find occasion, at which meetings they may make such ordinances and rules, not repugnant to or inconsistent with the laws of the Commonwealth, as to the greatest part of the inhabitants shall seem necessary and convenient for the good government of the

c. 2 Bioren 423. Power to make rules and ordinances.

---

c. This section was supplied by the Act of 16th March, 1803, (7 Bioren, pg. 34.)

8

said borough, and the same rules and orders to put in execution, and the same to revoke, alter and make new, as occasion shall require. And also to impose such rules and amercements upon breakers of the said ordinances, as to the makers thereof shall be thought reasonable, to be levied as above is directed in case of fines, for the use of the said borough; and also at the said meetings to mitigate or release the said fines, on the submission of the parties.

SEC. XII. And for the better preventing all encroachments, nuisances, contentions, annoyances and inconveniences, whatsoever, within the bounds and limits of the said borough, *Be it further enacted by the authority aforesaid*, That where any buildings have been heretofore erected within the original plan of said borough (other than such as have been erected unjustly on the out-lots) and shall happen to encroach on any of the said streets and alleys, or squares, such buildings shall not be deemed, held or taken for nuisances, or abateable as such. But to prevent a continuance of such encroachments, after such buildings shall be decayed, or require rebuilding, *Be it further enacted by the authority aforesaid*, That the owner or owners of such buildings shall not at any time rebuild on the street, lane, alley or square, so encroached on: And in case any person or persons shall rebuild on the said street, alley or square, so encroached on, the same shall be deemed, taken and judged, a public nuisance, and shall be abateable and punishable as such, and the person or persons so rebuilding shall forfeit and pay the sum of twenty pounds to the supervisors of the said streets, lanes, alleys and squares, to be applied towards repairing the same, being thereof first legally convicted in any county court of Quarter Sessions for the County of Berks.

SEC. XIII. And, to the intent that the streets, lanes, alleys, and such others as shall be hereafter laid out, may be duly regulated, made, and kept in good order, *Be it enacted by the authority aforesaid*, That no person or persons whatsoever shall, from and after the publication of this act, lay

Marginal notes:

Buildings heretofore erected, that encroach, not to be deemed nuisances;

but not to be rebuilt, nor future encroachments made.

2 Bioren 424. No foundation of any party wall to be laid by any person, before applying to the regulators, who are to be appointed by the Burgesses.

the foundation of any party wall, or front of any building, adjoining the streets, lanes and alleys, within the said borough, before they have applied to the surveyors or regulators, to be appointed by the Burgesses and Assistants of the said borough, who are hereby empowered, as often as there shall be occasion, to appoint three discreet persons to be surveyors or regulators of the said streets, lanes and alleys, so far as the same are already laid out and built upon, and of such streets, lanes and alleys, as shall hereafter from time to time be laid out and opened, by the owners of the ground within the said borough, respectively; which said persons, so to be appointed, shall direct the regulation of the said streets, lanes and alleys, and of the foot-way on the sides of the street, and fronting the houses and lots in the said borough, with the width or breadth of such foot-way; and, upon application made to them, shall regulate and lay out the proper gutters, channels and conduits, for the carrying off the water; and shall and may enter upon the lands of any person or persons, in order to set out the foundations, and to regulate the walls to be built between party and party, as to the breadth and thickness thereof; which foundations shall be equally laid upon the lands of the persons between whom such party wall is to be made; and the first builder shall be reimbursed one moiety of the charge of such party wall, or for so much thereof as the next builder shall have occasion to make use of, before such next builder shall any ways use or break into the said wall; and the charge or value thereof shall be set by the said regulators, or any two of them.

SEC. XIV. *And be it further enacted by the authority aforesaid,* That if any person or persons shall begin or lay a foundation of any party wall or building, before the place be viewed and directed by the said regulators, or any two of them, or otherwise than the same shall be set out and directed by the said regulators, every such person or persons, as well employers as master-builders, shall forfeit and pay the sum of five pounds, to the Burgesses of the said borough for

Owners not to build on the streets so encroached on.

the time being, or one of them, for the public use and benefit thereof, being of the said offence first convicted in the
county court of Quarter Sessions of the county of Berks.

SEC. XV. *Provided always, and be it further enacted,* That
if either party, between whom such foundation shall be laid
out, shall find themselves aggrieved by the order or direction of the said regulators, he, she or they may appeal to the
Justices at the next court of Quarter Session, to be held for
the said county, who shall finally adjust and settle the same,
and the costs of such appeal shall be paid as the same Court
shall direct.

*Persons find-
ing themselves
aggrieved, may
appeal.*

SEC. XVI. *And be it further enacted by the authority aforesaid,* That the said regulators or surveyors attending the
said service, for their trouble, shall be paid by the party or
parties concerned in such foundation, or erecting such party
wall, the sum of five shillings each.

*2 Bioren 425.
Regulators pay.*

SEC. XVII. *And be it further enacted by the authority aforesaid,* That the said surveyors or regulators, or any two of
them, shall have full power to regulate partition fences within the said borough; and where the adjoining parties do
improve or inclose their lots, such fences shall be made in
the manner generally used, and kept in repair at the equal
cost of the parties so that the price for making exceed not
fifty shillings for every hundred feet, unless the owners or
possessors, between whom such fence is or shall be erected,
do agree otherwise; and if either party, between whom such
partition fence is or shall be made, shall neglect or refuse to
pay his half part or moiety for the repairing or setting up
such partition fence, as aforesaid, that then the party, at
whose cost the same was so set up or repaired, may, if above
five pounds, have his action at law for the said moiety of
such costs, and if five pounds, or under, the same shall be
determined before either of the Burgesses of the said borough, or any Justice of the Peace of the said county, as in
cases of debts not exceeding five pounds.

*Who have pow-
er to regulate
partition fen-
ces.*

SEC. XVIII. *And be it further enacted by the authority afore-*

said, That the freeholders and others within the said borough, qualified by charter to elect Burgesses and Assistants, shall meet together on the third Monday in the month of May, one thousand seven hundred and eighty-four, and every year thereafter on the same day, at the Court House in the said borough, and then and there, by tickets in writing, between the hours of ten in the morning and four in the afternoon, choose two discreet and reputable freeholders of the said borough to be the supervisors of the highways, and two to be assessors, which said supervisors and assessors, when chosen, and returned in writing, under the hand of one of the Burgesses of the said borough, into the office of the clerk of the county court of Quarter Sessions for the said county, shall be the assessors for the said borough, and the supervisors of the streets, lanes, alleys, roads and highways thereof, for the ensuing year; and if any supervisor or assessor so elected, or otherwise appointed by virtue of this act, shall refuse to take upon himself the said office, he shall, for every such offence, forfeit and pay any sum not exceeding ten pounds, to be applied towards maintaining, amending, cleaning, and repairing the said streets, lanes, alleys and highways.

d. Freeholders to meet, and choose supervisors and assessors.

SEC. XIX. *And be it further enacted by the authority aforesaid,* That the said supervisors of the highways shall, at least five days before the third Monday in May, yearly and ever year, give public notice in writing, by affixing the same at the Court House in the said borough, that the freeholders and inhabitants thereof are to meet on that day, to elect assessors and supervisors for the said borough, according to the directions of this act.

e. 2 Bioren 426. Notice to be given of the election of assessors and supervisors.

SEC. XX. *And be it further enacted by the authority afore-*

---

d. By Act of 2d March, 1859, (P. L. 96) the office of Supervisor was abolished and that of Street Commissioner substituted, they being invested with all the power of the Supervisor under the Act of incorporation, except as modified by the Act of 1859.

e. Now regulated by the general election laws.

f. Supervisors and assessors to lay a tax.

said, That it shall and may be lawful for the said supervisors, together with the assessors aforesaid, for the time being, to lay a rate or rates in any one year, not exceeding one shilling in the pound, on the clear yearly value of the real and personal estates of all and every the freeholders and inhabitants within the said borough, to be employed for the amending, repairing and keeping clean, and in good order, the streets, lanes, alleys and highways aforesaid, agreeable to the true intent and meaning of this act. *Provided nevertheless,* That the said rate or assessment shall be laid according to the best of their skill and judgment, and as near as may be to the county assessment for other purposes, laid in pursuance of an act, entitled "An Act for raising county rates and levies," having due regard to every man's estate within the said borough, without favor or affection to any person whatsoever. And the said supervisors and assessors, and each of them, shall, before they take on themselves the

Qualifications to be taken by them.

duties enjoined and required by this act, take an oath or affirmation, respectively, to the effect following, that is to say, "That they will well and truly cause the rates and sums "of money by this act imposed, to be duly and equally as-"sessed and laid, to the best of their skill and knowledge, "and therein shall spare no person for favour or affection, "nor grieve any for hatred or ill-will ; and that they, and "each of them, the said assessors and supervisors, will dili-"gently attend, and faithfully execute their said offices, re-"spectively, during the time of their continuance therein,

By whom to be administered.

"according to the best of their abilities and judgment." Which oath or affirmation the Burgesses of the said borough, or any of them, or any of the Justices of the Peace of the said county of Berks, are hereby empowered and required to administer, and certify the same to the Clerk of the Ses-

---

f. The levying of the road tax was vested in the council by the Act of 19th February, 1863, (P. L. 55) and was continued in them by the Act of 2d April, 1867, (P. L. 657.)

sions of the Peace of the said county, to be by him filed among the records and papers of his office.

SEC. XXI. *And be it further enacted by the authority aforesaid,* That if any of the supervisors or assessors, as aforesaid chosen, shall refuse or neglect to take upon him or themselves the said office, respectively, or shall die, or remove out of the said borough, or if the freeholders and inhabitants of the said borough aforesaid shall neglect or refuse to elect or choose supervisors or assessors, as is herein before directed and appointed, then, and in every such case, it shall and may be lawful to and for the Burgesses and Assistants of the said borough, or any four of them, a Burgess being one and they are hereby enjoined and required, to appoint another supervisor or supervisors, assessor or assessors, in the room and stead of such supervisor or supervisors, assessor or assessors, so refusing, dying, or removing, as aforesaid ; which said supervisor or supervisors, assessor or assessors, so appointed, shall have the same powers and authorities, and shall be liable to the same penalities, as the supervisors or assessors so chosen by the inhabitants of the said borough, in pursuance of the direction of this act ; and that the supervisors and assessors shall have and receive, for their trouble in rating and assessing the said rate, three pence in every pound ; and the said supervisors shall have and receive six-pence in the pound for collecting the same, and four shillings each for every day they shall attend in overseeing, employing, and attending the workmen upon the public streets, lanes, alleys and highways, within the said borough.

g Supervisors or assessors dying, refusing, or neglecting to serve, others to be appointed by the Burgesses.
2 Bioren 427.

Supervisors and assessors pay.

SEC. XXII. *And be it further enacted by the authority aforesaid,* That the said supervisors, before they proceed to the collecting of the said rate, shall procure the same to be al-

h. The tax before collected to be allowed of by the Burgesses.

---

g. By general law all vacancies in the office of Assessor are filled by the County Commissioners.

h. The collection of all taxes is now vested in a tax collector elected at the annual spring election, and the collection thereof regulated by the Act of 25th June, 1885, (P. L. 187) but the Act does not alter or amend any regulations in the charter or its supplements, as to the collection of the taxes.

lowed by the Burgesses of the said borough, or one of them, and one or more of the Justices of the Peace of the said county of Berks; and if any person or persons, so rated and assessed, shall refuse to pay the sum or sums on him or them charged, and shall not enter his or their appeal at the next court of General Quarter Sessions, that it shall and may be lawful to and for the said supervisor or supervisors (having first obtained a warrant, under the hand and seal of one of the said Burgesses, or one of the Justices of the Peace aforesaid, who are hereby empowered and required to grant such warrant) to levy the same on the goods and chattels of the person or persons so refusing; and in case such person shall not, within three days next after such distress made, pay the sum or sums on him or her assessed, together with the charges of such distress, that then the said supervisors or supervisor may proceed to the sale of the goods distrained, rendering to the owner the overplus, if any shall remain in such sale, reasonable charges being first deducted. *Provided nevertheless*, That if any person or persons shall find him, her or themselves, aggrieved with such rate or assessment, it shall and may be lawful for the Justices of the Peace, at their next General Quarter Sessions, upon the petition of the party, to take such order therein, as to them shall appear just, and the same shall conclude and bind all parties; and the supervisors, in case of such appeal, shall forbear making distress, until the same be determined in the Quarter Sessions, in the manner herein directed and appointed.

2 Bioren 428. Goods of tenants, &c., liable to be distrained for the tax. Tenants may deduct the tax out of their rent.

SEC. XXIII. *And be it further enacted by the authority aforesaid,* That the tenant or tenants, or any other person residing on, or having the care of lands of persons not residing in the said borough his or their goods and chattels shall be liable to be distrained, in manner aforesaid, for the payment of the said tax.

SEC. XXIV. *And be it further enacted by the authority aforesaid,* That where any tenant shall, before the passing of this act, have taken on a lease for one or more years any lands or

tenements, and shall pay the said rate hereby imposed on
the said lands or tenements so leased, or shall have his or her
goods and chattels distrained for the same, in such case it
shall and may be lawful for the said tenant or tenants, or
other persons aforesaid, to deduct the tax so paid out of the
rent due, or to become due, or for the tenant or tenants, or
other persons aforesaid, to recover the same from the owner
or owners by action, together with costs of suit, in the same
manner that demands are recoverable in other cases. *Provided always,* That nothing herein contained shall make void
or alter any contract heretofore made between any landlord
and tenant, respecting the payment of the road tax, or any
usage or custom in respect to the tenant's paying the said
tax, now subsisting between landlord and tenant.

SEC. XXV. *And be it enacted by the authority aforesaid,* That
the said supervisors shall, and they are hereby required and
enjoined, as often as the said several streets, lanes, alleys and
highways, shall be out of repair or want cleaning, to hire
and employ a sufficient number of laborers, and the necessary carts or waggons, to work upon, open, amend, repair
and clean the same, and to carry off and remove any filth
mud or dirt, which shall be therein, in the most effectual
manner, and shall purchase all materials necessary for that
purpose, and oversee the said laborers, and take care that
the said streets, lanes, alleys and highways, be effectually
opened, amended, repaired and cleaned, agreeable to the regulations so made by the said regulators, according to the true
intent and meaning of this act.

Supervisors to repair the streets;

SEC. XXVI. And in order to enable the said supervisors
the more effectually to discharge their duty, *Be it enacted
by the authority aforesaid,* That it shall and may be lawful
for the supervisors aforesaid, or any other person or persons,
by his or their order and directions, to enter upon any lots
or lands adjoining to or lying near the said streets, lanes,
alleys and highways, and to cut or open such drains or
ditches through the same, as he or they shall judge neces-

and to enter up-on lands adjoin-ing, to cut drains or dit-ches for carry-ing off the water.

sary completely to carry off and drain the water from such streets, lanes, alleys and highways; provided the same be done with as little injury and damage as may be to the owners of such lot or land; which drains and ditches, so cut and opened, shall be kept open by the said supervisors, if necessary for amending and keeping clean, and in good order, the said streets, lanes, alleys and highways, or any or either of them, and shall not be stopped or filled up by the owner or owners of such lot or land, or any other person or persons whatsoever, under the penalty of five pounds for every such offence, to be paid and applied for and towards keeping in good order and repair the said streets, lanes, alleys and highways.

SEC. XXVII. *And be it further enacted by the authority aforesaid,* That all and every supervisor or supervisors aforesaid, who shall refuse or neglect to do and perform his or their duty, as directed by this act (not otherwise particularly provided for) shall be fined and pay the sum of three pounds for every such offence, to be recovered in a summary way before either of the Burgesses of the said borough, or any Justice of the Peace of the county residing in the said borough, and to be applied towards repairing and keeping clean, and in good order, the said streets, lanes, alleys and highways. *Provided always,* That if any such supervisor or supervisors shall conceive him or themselves aggrieved by the judgment of such Burgess or Justice, he may appeal to the next county court of General Quarter Sessions, who shall, on the petition of the party, take such order therein, as to them shall appear just and reasonable, and the same shall be conclusive to all parties.

2 Bioren 429.
Penalty on sup-
ervisors for
neg'ect of duty.

i. Supervisors
to produce fair
and just ac-
counts to the
Burgesses;

SEC. XXVIII. *And be it further enacted by the authority aforesaid,* That the person or persons who shall have served the office of supervisor or supervisors the preceding year, shall,

---

i. Although the Street Commissioners do not collect any taxes, they are required by the Act of 1863 (P. L. 55) to present to the Auditors their accounts for adjustment, as stated in this section; and may be required to swear to any or

on the first day of June yearly, or within six days after, make up and produce to the said Burgesses and Assistants, a fair and just accounts of all such sums of money by him or them expended on the said streets, lanes, alleys and high-ways, and of all sums of money by him or them received by virtue of any assessments, and of all fines and penalities which have come to their hands; which accounts shall be entered in a book to be provided for that purpose, and shall be at-tested on oath or affirmation by such supervisor or super-visors, if required by any three or more of the freeholders or inhabitants of the said borough. And the said Burgessess *who are to ad-just and settle* and Assistants, or any four of them, of which four a Burgess *the same.* shall be one, shall have full power to adjust and settle the said accounts; and to allow of such charges and sums only, as they shall think just and reasonable; and if there shall appear to be any money remaining in the hands of the said supervisor or supervisors, they shall, by order in writing, signed by them, direct the same to be paid to the succeed-ing supervisor or supervisors; but in case the said super-visor or supervisors shall be found in advance for monies expended, and shall have carefully collected the sums of money assessed and imposed by virtue of this act, then the said Burgesses and Assistants shall, in like manner, order the succeeding supervisors to repay and reimburse the same, as soon as a sufficient sum of money shall come to their hands: And if such supervisor or supervisors shall neglect or refuse to make up and produce fair and just accounts, as aforesaid, or, having made up and produced such accounts, shall neglect or refuse forthwith to pay the monies which he or they shall be ordered, as aforesaid, to pay, or shall not deliver up the books wherein such accounts shall be entered to their successors, it shall and may be lawful for either of

all of the bills they may have presented to the council during the preceeding year. It is the duty of the council, under the Act of 16th March, 1860, (P. L. 174,) to require them to give bond with security, in such sum as the council may fix, for the faithful performance of their duty : just as is now required of the Over-seers of the Poor.

18

the Burgesses of the said borough, or any Justice of the Peace, on complaint to him made by any two of the said Assistants, to commit such delinquent or delinquents to the county jail, until the same shall be done. *Provided always,* That if any supervisor shall think himself aggrieved by the settlement of his accounts, as aforesaid, he may (having first paid over to his successor or successors the balance found in his hands) appeal to the next court of Quarter Sessions, who shall, on the petition of the party, take such order therein, and give such relief, as to them shall seem just and reasonable, and the same shall conclude and bind all parties.

* * * * * * *

SEC. XXX. And whereas doubts have arisen, whether, according to the laws now in force, the Justices of the Peace residing within the said borough, and who are chargeable with, or rated to taxes, levies or rates, within the same, may lawfully act in any case relating to the said borough : *Be it therefore enacted by the authority aforesaid,* That it shall and may be lawful to and for the Justices of the Peace for the said borough, and all and every the Justice or Justices of the Peace of the county of Berks aforesaid, residing or being in the same, to make, do and execute all and every act or acts, matter or matters, thing or things, appertaining to their offices, as Justice or Justices of the Peace so far as the same relates to the laws for the relief, maintenance and settlement of poor persons, for passing and punishing of vagrants, for opening, amending and repairing the streets, lanes, alleys and highways, or to any other laws concerning taxes, levies or rates, notwithstanding any such Justice or Justices is or are rated or chargeable with the taxes, levies or rates, within the same borough.

SEC. XXXI. *Provided always, and be it enacted by the authority aforesaid,* That this act, or anything herein contained, shall not authorize or empower any Justice or Justices of the Peace, for or within the said borough, to act in the determination of any appeal to the Quarter Sessions of the Peace for the said County of Berks, from any order, matter

2 Bioren 430.
Magistrates empowered to act in all matters appertaining to their office.

2 Bioren 481.
Proviso, in determining appeals to the Quarter Sessions.

or thing, relating to the same borough, anything herein contained to the contrary in any wise notwithstanding.

Sec. XXXII. And whereas it hath frequently happened that persons, in digging cellars and building houses, have thrown the clay and dirt from their cellars, and the rubbish from their buildings, into the streets, lanes, alleys and highways, of the said borough, and by suffering the same to remain there, have rendered the streets, lanes and alleys, impassable: *Be it therefore enacted by the authority aforesaid,* That if any person or persons, in digging or making cellars, foundations and buildings, vaults, wells, sinks, drains, or other works or improvements, shall, after the publication of this act, cast or throw any dirt, earth, clay, stone or other matter, into any public street, lane, alley or highway, within the said borough, and shall keep or suffer such dirt, earth, clay, stone or other matter, to remain upon such street, lane, alley or highway, so as unnecessarily to incommode or annoy the inhabitants of the said borough, and shall not remove the same upon notice given to him, her or them, for that purpose, or by order of the Burgesses of the said borough, or either of them, or by the regulators aforesaid, or any two of them, every such person or persons so offending, and being thereof convicted before either of the Burgesses of the said borough, or any Justice of the Peace of the county aforesaid, shall forfeit, for every such offence, the sum of forty shillings, and shall pay the cost of removing the same.

Penalty on persons casting dirt, earth, &c., from their improvements,Into any public street, and not removing the same.

Sec. XXXIII. *And be it further enacted by the authority aforesaid,* That if any person or persons whatsoever shall cast or lay, or cause to be cast or laid, any shavings, mud, ashes, dung, or other filth or annoyance, on any pavement, street, lane or alley, within the said borough, and shall not remove the same, on notice given to him, her or them, by the Burgesses of the said borough, or either of them, or by the regulators aforesaid, or any two of them, every such person and persons so offending, and being thereof convicted before either of the Burgesses of the said borough, or before any Justice

Penalty on persons laying shavings,dung, &c., ou any pavements.

of the Peace of the county aforesaid, shall forfeit and pay,
for every such offence, the sum of twenty shillings, and shall
pay the cost of removing the same.

SEC. XXXIV. *And be it further enacted by the authority*
aforesaid, That if any person or persons, after the publication of this act, cast or throw out of any cart, wagon or other
carriage, any rubbish, dirt or earth, in any public street,
lane or alley of the said borough, save only in such parts and
places as shall be appointed and agreed on by the said regulators and supervisors aforesaid, or any three of them, every
such person and persons offending, and being thereof convicted before either of the Burgesses of the said borough, or
before any Justice of the Peace of the said county, shall forfeit, for every such offence, the sum of ten shillings, and shall
pay the costs of removing the same.

2 Bioren 432.
Penalty on c st-
ing rubbish in
any public
street.

SEC. XXXV. *And be it further enacted by the authority afore-*
said, That if any distiller, soap-boiler or tallow-chandler,
within the said borough, shall discharge any foul or nauseous
liquor from any still-house or work-shop, so that such liquor
shall pass into or along any of the said streets, lanes or alleys, or if any soap-boiler or tallow-chandler shall keep, collect or use, or cause to be kept, collected or used, in any of
the built parts of the said borough, any stale, putrid, or
stinking fat, grease, or other matter, or if any butcher shall
keep at or near his slaughter-house any garbage or filth
whatsoever, so as to annoy any neighbor or any other person whatsoever, he, she or they, so offending, and being thereof convicted before the Burgesses of the said borough, or
either of them, or before any Justice of the Peace of the said
county, shall forfeit and pay, for every such offence, the sum
of three pounds, together with the costs of the prosecution.

Distillers not
to discharge
nauseous liqu-
or so as to run
through the
streets.

SEC. XXXVI. *And be it further enacted by the authority*
aforesaid, That if any person or persons shall, after the publication hereof, presume to cast, carry, draw out or lay, any
dead carcass, or any excrement or filth from vaults, privies
or necessary-houses, and shall leave such carcass or filth,

Penalty on
persons leaving
carrion in any
uninclosed
grounds.

without burying the same a sufficient depth, in any uninclosed grounds within the limits of the said borough, or on or near any of the streets, lanes, alleys or highways aforesaid, every person or persons so offending, and being thereof convicted before either of the Burgesses of the said borough, or before any Justice of the Peace of the said county, shall forfeit, for every such offence, the sum of three pounds, and shall pay the costs of removing and burying such carcass, excrement or filth, in such place and manner as the Burgesses of the said borough, or either of them, or the said regulators or supervisors, or any two of them, shall direct or appoint.

SEC. XXXVII. *And be it further enacted by the authority aforesaid*, That if any person or persons whatsoever shall willfully stop or obstruct the passage of the waters of any of the common sewers, hereafter to be made within the said borough, he or they, so offending, shall forfeit, for every such offence, any sum not exceeding twenty shillings, and shall pay the costs of removing such obstruction.

Penalty on persons obstructing the common sewers.

SEC. XXXVIII. *And be it further enacted by the authority aforesaid*, That if any person or persons shall make any pavements or footway before their houses or lots in the said borough, of a greater width or breadth, or height, than allowed or directed by the surveyors or regulators, to be appointed by virtue of this act, or contrary to the directions of the said regulators, or any two of them, or shall set up posts in the streets, lanes or alleys aforesaid, or any of them, otherwise than as allowed and directed by the said regulators or any two of them, and shall refuse or neglect to take up, remove, or place the same in such manner as the said regulators, or any two of them, shall direct or order, after two days notice to him, her or them, for that purpose given, by order of the Burgesses of the said borough, or either of them, or by order of the said regulators, or any two of them, every such person so offending, and being thereof convicted before either of the Burgesses of the said borough, or before any Justice of the Peace of the county aforesaid, shall forfeit and

2 Bioren 433. Penalty on making any pavement or footway, &c. contrary to the directions of the regulators, &c.

pay the sum of thirty shillings for every such offence. And the said regulators, or any two of them, shall and may take up, regulate, pull down, remove and replace, such pavement and posts, in such manner as they shall think proper, and the costs of taking up, regulating, pulling down, removing and replacing such pavements and posts, shall be paid by the party or parties so offending in the premises.

SEC: XXXIX. *And be it further enacted by the authority aforesaid,* That if any person or persons shall hereafter make

Regulation relating to encroachments by cellar-doors.

and set up, or cause to be made and set up, in any street of fifty feet wide or upwards, within the said borough, any porch, cellar-door or step, which shall extend beyond the distance of four feet and three inches into such street, or a proportionate distance into any narrower street, except in Penn street, where the steps shall not exceed six feet, and in the main square, where the steps shall not exceed eight feet; and if any person or persons shall hereafter make and set up, or cause to be made and set up, any bulk, jut-window, or incumbrance whatsoever, whereby any passage of any street, lane or alley, shall be obstructed, or shall place, or cause to be placed, any spout or gutter, whereby the passage of any street, lane or alley, shall be incommoded, every person so offending, and being thereof convicted before the Burgesses of the said borough, or before any Justice of the Peace of the county aforesaid, shall, for every such offence, forfeit and pay the sum of thirty shillings, and shall forthwith remove the said nuisance, or cause the same to be removed; and on failure thereof, by the space of three days next after notice to him, her or them, for that purpose given, by order of the Burgesses of the said borough, by the said regulators, or any two of them, then, and in that case, the regulators aforesaid, or any of them, shall and may remove the same, or cause the same to be removed; and the costs and expenses attending such removal shall be paid by the party or parties so offending.

SEC. XL. *And be it further enacted by the 'authority afore-*

23

said, That the owner or owners of every house within the said borough, having, at the publication hereof, any porch, cellar-door or step, extending into any street beyond the limits aforesaid, or having fixed or fastened to such house any bulk, jut-window, or other incumbrance whatsoever, shall, yearly and every year, pay to the supervisors of the said streets, lanes, alleys and highways, to be applied towards repairing and amending the same, such sum or sums of money as the said Burgesses and Assistants shall assess, until such porch, cellar-door or step, to him, her or them, respectively, belonging, shall be reduced to the limits aforesaid, or such bulk, jut-window, or other incumbrance, shall be removed and taken away; and every owner or owners of any house or houses, whereunto any spouts or gutters shall, at the time of the publication hereof, be so fixed or placed, that the waters thereby discharged may incommode persons passing in the streets, lanes or alleys, shall, and they are hereby enjoined and required, forthwith to remove, or effectually to alter and amend the same.

2 Bloren 434. Owners of porches, &c., exceeding the above limitation, to be assessed, till reduced or taken away.

SEC. XLI. *And be it enacted by the authority aforesaid*, That if any person or persons, after the publication of this act, shall wilfully or maliciously remove, misplace, or injure any pipes or trunks already fixed or placed, or that may or shall be hereafter fixed or placed, by the direction of the Burgesses and Assistants of the said borough, or conveying water to, from, or through any part of the said borough, or if any person or persons shall willfully or maliciously, without the consent and direction of the Burgesses and Assistants aforesaid, by any ways or means whatsoever, obstruct or prevent the course of such waters in or through any such trunks, pipes or conduits, as are, or shall, or may be placed as aforesaid, or shall spoil or injure any cistern, which shall or may be placed for the reception of such water, every person so offending, and being thereof legally convicted before the Burgesses of the said borough, or either of them, or before any Justice of the Peace for the county aforesaid, shall for-

Penalty on persons removing or damaging the pipes or trunks for conveying water.

feit and pay the sum of five pounds for every such offence, and shall pay the costs of repairing and putting such trunks, pipes, conduits or cisterns, in good order and repair.

Sec. XLII. And whereas it hath been usual for the merchants and traders, within the said borough, to keep large quantities of gunpowder in their dwelling houses and shops, to the great and manifest danger of the inhabitants: *Be it therefore enacted by the authority aforesaid,* That no person or persons whatsoever, within the limits of said borough, shall, from and after the publication of this act, keep in any house, shop, cellar, store or other place, within the said borough, No persons to keep more than 25lb. of gun-powder in their houses. any more or greater quantity than twenty-five pounds weight of gunpowder, which shall be kept in the highest story of the house, at any one time, unless it be at least fifty yards from any dwelling house, under the penalty of ten pounds.

2 Bioren 435, Manner of re-covering and applying fines. Sec. XLIII. *And be it further enacted by the authority aforesaid,* That all the penalties, fines and forfeitures, herein before imposed by this act, the manner of levying and recovering of which is not before directed, not exceeding the sum of five pounds, shall be recovered before one of the Burgesses of the said borough, or before one of the Justices of the Peace of and for the said county of Berks, and shall be levied by warrant, under the hand and seal of such Burgess or Justice, directed to any constable of said borough or county, who is hereby empowered and required to execute the same, by distress and sale of the goods and chattels of the offender; and where goods and chattels sufficient cannot be found, then the party or parties so offending shall be committed to the common goal of the said county, there to remain until payment made, or until discharged by due course of law; and if such penalties, fines and forfeitures, shall exceed the sum of five pounds, then to be recovered by action of debt, bill, plaint or information, in any county court within this State, wherein no essoin, protection, or wager of law, nor more than one imparlance, shall be allowed; and all fines and forfeitures arising by this act, not herein before appropriated, shall

be paid to the supervisors of the streets, alleys and highways, to be employed in mending and repairing the same.

SEC. XLIV. *And be it enacted by the authority aforesaid,* That nothing in a certain act of Assembly, passed in the year of our Lord one thousand seven hundred and seventy-two, entitled "An Act for opening, and better amending and keep-"ing in repair, the public roads and highways within this "province," shall be deemed, construed or taken, to extend to the public roads, streets, lanes or alleys, within the said borough, or to the assessing the inhabitants thereof for the purposes therein mentioned, or to any other matter or thing to be done or performed therein, but the said act, so far as it respects or relates to said borough, and no further, is hereby declared to be repealed.

The act relating to public roads and highways not to extend to the borough of Reading.

SEC. XLV. *And be it also enacted by the authority aforesaid,* That if any person or persons be sued or prosecuted for any thing done in pursuance of this act, he, she or they may plead the general issue, and give this act, and the special matter, in evidence, for their justification ; and if the plaintiff prosecutor become nonsuit, or suffer a discontinuance, or a verdict pass against him, the defendant shall have treble costs, to be recovered as in cases where costs by law are given to defendants.

Passed 12th September, 1783.

A SUPPLEMENT to the act, entitled "An Act to erect the town of Sunbury, in the County of Northumberland into a borough."

SECTION I. *Be it enacted by the Senate and House of Representatives of the Commonwealth of Pennsylvania, in General Assembly met, and it is hereby enacted by the authority of the same,* That from and after the passing of this act, similar rights, privileges and immunities, as are now exercised, holden and enjoyed, by the Burgesses, freeholders and inhabitants of the Borough of Reading, in and by the ninth

An additional privilege of markets and faire granted to the inhabitants of the borough of Sunbury.

section of the act, establishing the said borough, shall and may from henceforth, be exercised, holden and enjoyed, by the Burgesses, freeholders and inhabitants of the Borough of Sunbury, in the County of Northumberland; and the yearly fairs in the said Borough of Sunbury, shall commence on the Tuesday following the fairs holden in the Borough of Reading.

Passed 22d January, 1803—P. L. 19,

A further SUPPLEMENT to the act, entitled "An Act to erect the Town of Sunbury in the County of Northumberland into a borough."

Whereas the Burgesses and sundry inhabitants of the Borough of Sunbury, in the County of Northumberland, by their petition to the legislature, have suggested certain alterations and amendments of the existing acts of incorporation of the said borough, whereby the same would be rendered more conformable to the wishes and convenience of the said inhabitants: Therefore,

a. The qualified inhabitants of the borough of Sunbury shall annually elect eight common councilmen, each of whom to take an oath of office before he enters on the duties thereof.

SECTION I. *Be it enacted by the Senate and House of Representatives of the Commonwealth of Pennsylvania, in General Assembly met, and it is hereby enacted by the authority of the same,* That the inhabitants of the said borough, qualified to vote for Burgesses and Assistants, shall at the same time and place at which Burgesses and Assistants are elected, annually elect eight inhabitants of the said borough qualified as aforesaid, to serve as common councilmen, each of whom before he enters on the duties of his office, shall take an oath or solemn affirmation, before some Judge or Justice of the Peace of the said county, well and faithfully to execute the office of a common councilman of the said borough.

Powers of the Burgesses, assistants and common councilmen.

SEC. II. *And be it further enacted by the authority aforesaid,* That the said Burgesses, Assistants and common council-

---

a. By Act 2d March, 1859, P. L. 96, all of this Act after the words "as occasion may require" in the second section was repealed.

men, in common council assembled, shall have full power and authority to frame all laws and ordinances, necessary and convenient for the government and welfare of the said borough, and the same at their discretion to revoke, alter and make anew, as occasion may require, reserving nevertheless to the inhabitants at large, duly qualified as aforesaid, in their town meetings, to revoke, alter and amend the said laws and ordinances : *Provided*, That a majority of the whole number of the said inhabitants concur in such revocation, alteration or amendments.

Proceedings before the laws and ordinances of the corporation are to have effect, and for revoking or altering the same.

SEC. III. *And be it further enacted by the authority aforesaid*, That in order to give due notice of such laws and ordinances, and that a full opportunity may be had for the inhabitants aforesaid, to revoke, alter or amend the same, the said laws shall be published for ten days before they shall obtain any operation, and in the interval a town meeting shall be convened by the Burgesses and Assistants, and if at such town meeting a sufficient number of the inhabitants shall not appear to revoke or alter the said laws or ordinances, or appearing shall not revoke, or alter the same, the said laws and ordinances shall at the expiration of the said ten days become of full force and effect, subject nevertheless to revocation, alteration or amendment by the said common council, or by a majority of the whole number of inhabitants duly qualified as aforesaid, at any subsequent town meeting.

Passed 16th March, 1803.—P. L. 367.

———

A N ACT authorizing the chief burgess of the borough of Sunbury to sell and convey a portion of the bank of the river opposite said borough, &c.

SEC. 1. *Be it enacted &c.*, That the chief burgess of the borough of Sunbury, in the county of Northumberland, and his successors, be, and he is hereby authorized, at such times and in such manner as may be directed by the bur-

Burgess of Sunbury authorized to sell a

28

portion of the bank of the river.

a.

Proviso.

gess and town council of said borough, for the time being to sell and convey in fee simple, to such person or persons as may become the purchaser or purchasers of the same, for the purpose of constructing warves, so much of the bank of the river Susquehanna, opposite Broadway, in said borough, as may be directed by the said burgess and town council: *Provided,* That said wharves shall not be extended into the river further than one hundred feet from from the top of the bank.

Approved April 3rd, 1837, P. L. 262

An Act to authorize the construction of an embankment for the protection of the Borough of Sunbury, &c., and for other purposes.

Borogh of Sunbury and supervisors of Augusta township, authorized to construct an embankment.

SECTION I. *Be it enacted by the Senate and House of Representatives of the Commonwealth of Pennsylvania, in General Assembly met, and it is hereby enacted by the authority of the same,* That the corporation of the Borough of Sunbury, and the supervisors of the township of Augusta, or such persons as the said borough and supervisors shall authorize, shall have power to construct an embankment on the land belonging to the estate of the late Thomas Grant, deceased, and to use the said embankment for a public road, if advisable.

Power to enter upon lands.

SEC. II. That the said corporation, or supervisors or citizens, shall have power to enter upon and over so much of the land lying contiguous to the said embankment, and to use such materials as may be necessary for the construction of said embankment, first paying the owner or owners, the full value thereof, or give security for the payment of the same ; and for the purpose of ascertaining the amount thereof, if the parties cannot agree upon the same, either party

Damages to be first paid.

---

a. It is doubtful whether this act conferred any power of conveyance on the corporate authorities.

may petition the Court of Common Pleas of Northumberland county, setting forth the facts, praying for the appointment of viewers to assess the damages, (if any ;) whereupon, How to be ascertained. the said court shall appoint three disinterested persons, who shall examine the premises and assess the damages, after being first duly sworn, and make return to said court ; which report, upon being approved by said court, shall be final and conclusive ; and the amount hereof, together with the costs of said proceeding, shall be paid by said borough and said How paid. township, in equal proportions, by an order drawn on their respective treasurers.   *   *   *   *   *   *

Approved 22d April, 1846, P. 492.

AN ACT * * *to extend the limits of the borough of Sunbury.* * * *

SEC. 13. *Be it enacted &c.*, That so much of the farm or Borough of Sunbury, limits extended. tract of land lately owned by Mrs. Sarah Gobin and Susan Scott, as lies west of the ravine commonly called the Gut, and so much of the farm late the estate of Samuel Hunter, deceased, as lies west of the said Gut, be and are hereby annexed to and included within the corporate limits of the borough of Sunbury : *Provided*, That the right of fer- Proviso. riage on the Susquehanna river adjoining said lands, be and remain in the owners of the same, and within the limits of Sunbury so extended. * * *

Approved April 19th, 1853 P. L. 589.

A further SUPPLEMENT to an Act to erect the Town of Sunbury, in the County of Northumberland, into a borough.

WHEREAS, The Burgesses, Town Councils and sundry in- Preamble. habitants of the said borough, are desirous of having certain alterations, amendments and additions to the existing acts of incorporation and the supplements thereto, of the said borough, whereby the same would be rendered more comformable to the wishes of the said inhabitants ; therefore,

SECTION I. *Be it enacted by the Senate and House of Representatives of the Commonwealth of Pennsylvania, in General Assembly met, and it is hereby enacted by the authority of the same,* That the Burgesses, Assistant Burgess and common council, in town council assembled, shall have full power and authority to require and direct the grading, curbing, paving and guttering of the side or foot walks by the owner or owners of the lots of ground respectively fronting on any of the public streets or highways of said borough, in accordance with such regulations as may be presented by the said town council.

Powers of Burgess and town council relative to curbing, paving, &c.

ARTICLE I.

To cause the same to be done on failure of the owner or owners thereof within the time prescribed by ordinance, and to collect the cost of the work and material, with twenty per cent. advance thereon, from said owner or owners, as claims are by law recoverable under the provisions of the law relative to mechanics' liens ; and the particulars of such labor and materials, the name or names of the actual or reputed owner or owners, as also of the occupier or occupiers of the premises, for the time being, shall be set forth in a statement to be filed within thirty days after such work shall have been finished. The town council shall have the authority to regulate the roads, streets, lanes, alleys, courts, common sewers, public squares, common grounds, footwalks, pavements, gutters, culverts and the heights, grades, widths, slopes and forms thereof, and they shall have other needful jurisdiction over the same.

Council authorized to regulate roads, streets, &c.

SEC. II. To make regulations relative to the cause and management of fires, and within such limits within the borough as they may deem proper to prescribe, and to authorize the borough authorities to appropriate money for the purchase of fire engines, and to fire companies.

Regulations relative fires and fire apparatus.

SEC. III. To levy and collect, annually, for borough pur-

31

poses, and also for the purpose of liquidating the debt of the borough, any tax not exceeding one half cent on the dollar, on the valuation assessed for county purposes, as is now or may be provided by law; all property, offices, professions and persons made taxable by the laws of this Commonwealth for county rates and levies, shall be taxable after the same manner for borough purposes.

a. Taxes, levying and collection of.

Sec. IV. It shall be the duty of the Chief Burgess to issue his warrant for the collection of all taxes assessed for borough purposes, and to demand and receive sufficient security, in the amount fixed by the corporation, from the treasurer, (who shall be appointed by the town council) collector and high constable.

Chief Burgess to issue warrant for collection of taxes.

Sec. V. The Chief Burgess is hereby authorized to issue his precepts, as often as occasion may require, to the collector or collectors of the borough, (who shall be appointed in the same manner as the borough treasurer,) commanding him or them to collect all taxes assessed for the use of said borough, and the same to pay over to the treasurer thereof, which collector or collectors shall have the same power that collectors now have in collecting county rates and levies.

To issue precept to collectors, &c.

Sec. VI. The collector of borough taxes may be proceeded against, by the borough treasurer, in the same manner for neglect to pay over the amount of his duplicate according to law, as provided in the case of collectors of county rates and levies.

Collector of taxes, how proceeded against.

Sec. VII. The town council shall constitute a court of appeal, and prior to the collection of any borough tax, the collector shall inform each inhabitant of the amount of his tax, and of the time and place of appeal: *Provided,* That the court of appeal shall have no other power, as such, than to determine the apportionment of said taxes, and to remedy any grievance that may occur.

Council to constitute a board of appeal.

Sec. VIII. All bills shall first be passed by the town coun-

a. The maxium tax rate was raised to ten mills by Act of September, 1867, P. L. 657.

Bills to be passed upon by town council. cil, and after the same shall have been so passed, the chief burgess shall draw his order on the borough treasurer for the same, attested by the town clerk, except bills for the relief of paupers, which shall be paid by the treasurer on orders from Overseers of the Poor.

Relief of paupers.

Officers, when and where elected. SEC. IX. The following officers shall be elected on the third Friday of March, in each and every year, after this supplement shall have become a law, at the time and place now provided by the act of incorporation to which this is a supplement, viz: Two Burgesses, (one of whom shall be Chief Burgess as is now regulated by the act of incorporation;) four Assistant Burgesses; eight Common Councilmen; one High Constable; one Town Clerk; one Judge, and two Inspectors of the general election; one Assessor, and two Assistant Assessors when required by the laws of this Commonwealth; two Overseers of the Poor, and two Commissioners of streets, lanes and alleys.

b. Power of commissioners of streets. SEC. X. The Commissioners of streets, lanes and alleys, shall have the same power and authority as is vested in the supervisors by the act of incorporation to which this is a supplement; and the said office of supervisor is hereby abolished, and the duties appertaining thereto shall be performed by the said Commissioners, save and except so much of the same as is altered and supplied by this supplement: *Provided,* That the said Commissioners shall be under the direction and control of the town council.

Proviso.

Salaries to be fixed by town council. SEC. XI. The amount to be paid for the collection of taxes, the salaries of Chief Burgess, Town Clerk, High Constable, Assessors, Auditors, Street Commissioners, Overseers of the Poor, and Treasurer, shall be fixed by the Town Council.

SEC. XII. Three borough auditors shall be appointed by the Town Council, to serve for the term of one year from the

---

b. The borough officers have been changed by subsequent Acts, and by the division of the borough into five wards. See note on charter, and decree of division into wards *post.*

time of their appointment, whose duty it shall be to audit, adjust and settle the accounts of the officers above stated.

SEC. XIII. The Town Council shall have power to establish a nightly watch and special police whenever they may see proper so to do, whose compensation shall be fixed by the said Town Council.

SEC. XIV. All persons entitled to vote for members of the legislature, and who shall have resided in the borough for the space of one year, as is provided for in the act of incorporation, shall be entitled to vote for all the offices herein set forth

SEC. XV. The Town Council are hereby authorized to change the names of the different streets, lanes and alleys of the borough, whenever they may deem it proper so to do.

SEC. XVI. That all that part of the second section of a supplement to the act, entitled "An Act to erect the Town of Sunbury, in the County of Northumberland, into a borough," approved the sixteenth day of March, eighteen hundred and three, after the word "require," and section third of the same supplement, be and are hereby repealed.

SEC. XVII. That such parts of the act of incorporation and laws of said borough, and supplements thereto, as conflict with this supplement, be and the same are hereby repealed.

SEC. XVIII. The first election under this supplement shall be held on the third Friday of March, A. D. eighteen hundred and fifty-nine, at the time and place of holding the election for inspectors of the general election.

Approved March 2d, 1859.—P. L. 96.

c. Borough auditors, how appointed.
Night watch.
Who entitled to vote d.
Council may change names of streets.
Repeal.
Repeal.
First election, when to be held.

_____

c. Borough Auditors are now elected at the annual spring election, as provided by the Acts regulating the division of the borough into wards (see Act of 10th May, 1878, P. L. 51.) The Auditors possess all the power of auditing and settling accounts conferred on the Burgesses by the charter, or on Auditors by this or subsequent Acts.

d. Under the new constitution any qualified voter may now vote for borough officers.

AN ACT to change the limits of the borough of Sunburg, in the county of Northumberland.

SECTION 1. *Be it enacted. &c.*, That so much of the thirteenth section of the act of the nineteenth day of April, Anno Domini one thousand eight hundred and fifty-three, entitled "An Act for the relief of Jacob Housman, Barbara Widow, et cetera," annexed to and included within the corporate limits of the borough of Sunbury, part of the farms or tracts of land lately owned by Mrs. Sarah Gobin and Susan Scott, and late of the estate of Samuel Hunter, deceased, be and the same is hereby repealed : and the said parts of said farms or tracts of land shall be and the same are hereby re-annexed to the township of Upper Augusta, in the county of Northumberland, and shall hereafter comprise a part of the territory of the said township of Upper Augusta, as fully and effectually as if the same had never been included within the limits of the borough of Sunbury.

Approved April 2nd, 1860, P. L. 522.

Re-annexes, Hunter and Scott forms to Upper Augusta. (margin note)

A further SUPPLEMENT to an act to erect the town of Sunbury, in the County of Northumberland into a borough, passed the twelfth day of September, Anno Domini one thousand seven hundred and eighty three.

SECTION 1. *Be it enacted by the Senate and House of Representatives of the Commonwealth of Pennsylvania in General Assembly met, and it is hereby enacted by the authority of the same,* That the burgesses, assistant burgesses and common councils of the borough of Sunbury, in town council assembled, shall have full power and authority to levy and collect, annually, as borough taxes therein are now levied and collected for road and poor purposes, road and poor taxes not exceeding one cent on the dollar, upon all real and personal estate, which, by existing laws, is taxable for road and poor purposes, on the valuation assessed for county purposes ; and the accounts of the treasurer, and of all collec-

Burgess and councilmen authorized to levy and collect road and poor taxes. (margin note)

tors of taxes and other officers, shall be audited in the manner and as provided in the act to which this supplement, and the supplements thereto.

Section 2. That the election within the borough of Sunbury, for officers, as provided by existing laws, shall be held on the third Friday of February, hereafter, and one person shall be elected to fill the office of chief burgess, and one person to fill the office of second burgess, to be voted for on seperate tickets; and all laws inconsistent herewith are hereby repealed.

Time of holding borough election.

Chief and Second Burgess to be elected.

Repeal.

Approved February 19th, 1863, P. L. 55.

A further SUPPLEMENT to an act to erect the town of Sunbury, in the county of Northumberland, into a borough.

Section 1. *Be it enacted by the Senate and House of Representatives of the Commonwealth of Pennsylvania in General Assembly met, and it is hereby enacted by the authority of the same,* That the burgess and councilmen of the borough of Sunbury shall have full power and authority to appoint a town clerk and high constable, in and for the said borough of Sunbury, in case the said offices have been, or shall hereafter become, vacant, by reason of the death, resignation, of the persons elected thereto; and also in case of failure of the electors, in said borough, to elect persons to fill the same.

Burgess and council may appoint a town clerk and high constable, in case of a vacancy.

Section 2. That the chief burgess of said borough shall have full power and authority to enforce all by-laws and rules of order, adopted by the town council of said borough, on the tenth day of July, Anno Domino one thousand eight hundred and fifty-five; and he is hereby authorized to issue his precept, under the seal of said corporation, as often as occasion may require, directed to the high constable of said borough, commanding him to collect all fines and penalties, imposed by virtue of said by-laws, and cause the same to be paid to the treasurer of said borough.

Burgess authorized to enforce by-laws, regulations, &c.

Approved March 17th, 1865, P. L. 407.

AN ACT to legalize the action of the chief burgess and town council of the borough of Sunbury, in the county of Northumberland, in the appropriation of money for county purposes.

SECTION I. *Be it enacted by the Senate and House of Representatives of the Commonwealth of Pennsylvania in General Assembly met, and it is hereby enacted by the authority of the same,* That the action of the chief burgess and town council of the borough of Sunbury, in the county of Northumberland, in appropriating the sum of five thousand dollars toward the costs and expense of the erection of a new court house, in the said borough of Sunbury, is hereby legalized and made valid and binding; and said authorities shall have power and are hereby required to levy and collect, as other borough taxes are levied and collected, a tax sufficient to pay the said sum of five thousand dollars; and that they are hereby required to pay the same into the treasury of Northumberland county, for the use of said county, on, or before, the first day of May, Anno Domini one thousand eight hundred and sixty-six.

Approved April 5th, 1866, P. L. 532.

Donation of $5000.00 to new Court House legalized.

A further SUPPLEMENT to an act to erect the borough of Sunbury, in the county of Northumberland, into a borough.

SECTION 1. *Be it enacted &c.,* That from and after the passage of this act the borough of Sunbury, in the county of Northumberland, shall be divided into two wards, as follows, namely: All that portion of the said borough lying east of the Northern Central railroad, shall be called the East ward, and the remainder shall be called the West ward.

Borough divided into two wards.

SEC. 2. That the East and West wards shall from and after the passage of this act, form two seperate election districts; and the qualified voters therein shall hereafter, seperately, [elect], on the third Friday of February next, and on the same day, in every year thereafter. elect two assis-

To form two seperate election districts.

Election of officers.

tant burgesses and four councilmen, one assessor, one judge
and two inspectors to conduct the general and borough
elections in said wards, and at such times as are directed
by the existing laws of this commonwealth, a constable
and two justices of the peace in each of said wards, and all
such other officers as are allowed to the boroughs, or townships, in this county.

SEC. 3. That for the purpose of conducting the next gen- *Officers appoint-ed to hold first election.*
eral and ward elections, to be held in October and Febru-
ary next, for the East and West wards of said borough,
held under the provisions of this act, Jacob H. Engle is
hereby appointed judge, and William Hendricks and Rob-
ert Farnsworth inspectors of the East ward elections, and
Alexander Mantz is hereby appointed judge, and George
B. Youngman and Philip Clark inspectors of the West
ward elections.

SEC. 4. That it shall be the duty of the commissioners *County commis-sioners to furn-ish ballot boxes.*
of the county of Northumberland to furnish, to the judges
and inspectors of each of the said wards, the same ballot
boxes, blank forms, list of taxable and other matters, as are
now furnished to judges and inspectors of elections in said
county.

SEC. 5. That all officers, now holding office in the said *Certain officers to continue.*
borough, shall continue to act as officers of said borough
until the expiration of their terms of office.

SEC. 6. That the county commissioners shall provide *Rooms for hold-ing elections.*
seperate rooms, in the court house in said borough, for the
purpose of holding general and borough elections therein.

SEC. 7. That for the protection of said borough from *Burgess, &c., authorized to have a river bank construct-ed along Front street.*
floods in the river Susquehanna, the burgesses, assistant
burgess and common council, in town council assembled,
shall have full power and authority to cause to be made
and constructed a river bank upon, or along, the public
highway in said borough, called Front street, formerly
Broadway, of such height, form, slope and grade as the
said town council may direct; and all work, and contracts

Certain work, &c., heretofore done, declared valid.

Town council authorized to pay for same.

Certain orders heretofore drawn, declared valid.

for work and materials, which the said town council have heretofore done, and made, for and about the erection and construction of a river bank in, upon or along, said street, is hereby made to be valid and binding, and the said town council are hereby authorized and empowered to pay, or cause to be paid, all sums of money which may have been heretofore contracted for the grading and erection of such river bank; and all orders heretofore drawn by the chief burgess, and attested by the town clerk, on the borough treasurer, for the payment of money for work, labor and materials, heretofore contracted for by the civil engineer selected by the said council, and duly agreed and assented to by the chief burgess, in pursuance of any resolution of the town council, for and about the erection and construction of said river bank, are hereby declared to be valid and binding; and the borough treasurer is hereby authorized

Borough treasurer authorized to pay.

and empowered to pay the said orders, out of any moneys that may be in his hands for borough purposes.

Town council authorized to levy and collect annually, certain t.xes.

SEC. 8. The said town council shall have power and authority to levy and collect, annually, for borough purposes, and also for the purpose of liquidating the debt of the borough, any tax not exceeding ten mills on the dollar, for road purposes, any tax not exceeding ten mills on the dollar, and for poor purposes, any tax not exceeding ten mills on the dollar, on the valuation assessed for county purposes, as is now, or may be provided by law and all property, offices, professions and persons made taxable, by the

Subjects of taxation.

laws of this commonwealth, for the county rates and levies, shall be taxable after the same manner for borough, road and poor purposes.

Town council authorized to borrow money.

Limitation.

May issue bond.

SEC. 9. That for the purpose of funding the debt of the borough, and for other borough purposes, as the town council may direct, the said town council are hereby authorized and empowered to borrow any sum, or sums, of money, not exceeding, in the aggregate, the sum of fifty thousand dollars, and may issue bonds therefor, in the corporate name of the borough, payable at such times as the said town council may direct, not more than ten years after date, with rate of interest not exceeding seven per cent, payable semi-annually, and which bonds shall not be taxable for borough purposes; the said bonds shall be signed by the chief burgess and attested by the town clerk.

Interest.

Not to be taxable for borough purpose.

SEC. 10. And that an act, approved the second day of April, Anno Domini one thousand eight hundred and sixty, entitled "An Act to change the limits of the borough of Sunbury, in the county of Northumberland," and that all laws or parts of laws, inconsistent with the provisions of this act, are hereby repealed.

Repeal.

Approved April 2nd, 1867, P. L. 657.

A SUPPLEMENT to an act to divide the borough of Sunbury into two wards, approved April second, one thousand eight hundred and sixty seven.

SECTION 1. *Be it enacted &c.*, That the first section of the act, to which this is a supplement, shall read as follows, to wit: That from and after the passage of this act the borough of Sunbury, in the county of Northumberland, shall be divided into two wards as follows, namely: All that portion of said borough lying east of the Northern Central railroad and the Philadelphia and Erie railroad, shall be called the East ward, and the remainder shall be called the West ward.

Redefines ward boundaries.

Approved March 26th, 1868, P. L. 508.

AN ACT authorizing the burgess and council of the borough of Sunbury, in Northumberland county to open and extend Second street and Fourth street, in said borough.

SEC. 1. *Be it enacted &c.*, That David Rockefeller, Abraham Shipman, Charles C. Hay, Christian Neff, Henry Feg-

Certain persons appointed com-

missioners to extend Second and Fourth streets. ley, David Fry, or a majority of them, are hereby appointed commissioners to view, lay out and extend Second street, in the borough of Sunbury, in Northumberland county, north-west from its present termination at Race street to the northern boundary of said borough, and southward from its present termination at ———— street, to the south-

a. ern boundary of said borough, in a line with said Second street, as nearly straight as can be done, having regard to the nature of the ground and agreeable to the recognized plan or plot of said borough, and the additions thereto ; also to lay out and extend Fourth street, in said borough, northward from its present termination to the northern boundary of said borough, in a line with said Fourth street, as nearly straight as can be done, having regard to the nature of the ground and the recognized plan or plot of said borough, and the additions thereto as aforesaid.

SEC. 2. It shall be the duty of said commissioners, or a Duties of commissioners. majority of them, first taking an oath or affirmation before a justice of the peace of said borough of Sunbury to perform the duties enjoined upon them by this act with impartaility and fidelity, to proceed, as soon after the passage of this act as they conveniently can, to attend to the duties specified in the preceeding section of this act; and they shall make out a plot-or draft of said streets, so to be opened as aforesaid, by their courses and distances, having regard to to the best ground and doing the least possible damage to property ; and they shall also make report of the width of said Second street and said Fourth street, and make return of the same, under their hands and seals, or the hands and seals of a majority of them, to the court of quarter sessions of Northumberland county, to be entered of record by the clerk of said court ; and thereupon the said Second street and the said Fourth street shall become public high-Duty of burgess and council. ways; and the burgesses and council of said borough of

---

a. The passage of this act was wholly unnecessary as the general road laws apply to the borough, and are better than any special law.

Sunbury are hereby authorized and empowered, and it shall be their duty, to cause the street commissioners of said borough to proceed forthwith to open said Second street and the said Fourth street: *Provided*, If, in the opinion of the burgesses and council of the said borough, it is not expedient to extend and open said Second street at the present, further north than a street marked on the plot or plan of Joseph W. Cake's addition to the said borough of Sunbury, as Joseph street, then they shall forthwith proceed to cause said Second street to be opened and extended to said Joseph street, and shall have power and authority to further open and extend said Second street to the northern boundary of said borough, as aforesaid, from time to time, as, in the opinion of the burgesses and councils of said borough, the growth and interests of said borough may demand and require.

Sec. 3. The court of quarter sessions of Northumberland county, on the petition of any owner of a lot of ground, or any owner of land through which the said streets shall or may be extended and opened, representing that he, she or they has or have sustained damage thereby, shall appoint six disinterested citizens of said borough of Sunbury, to view the premises and adjudge the amount of damages, if any, taking into consideration the advantages or disadvantages of the said street or streets to the complainant or complainants; and the said damages, so assessed and adjudged, after being approved by the court, shall be paid out of the treasury of said borough of Sunbury: *Provided always*, That said viewers shall each of them, before they proceed to assess such damages, take an oath or affirmation before some justice of the peace of said borough of Sunbury, justly and truely to value the same and to consider the advantages as well as the disadvantages of the extention and opening of said street to the complainant or complainants. *Damages, relative to.*

Sec. 4. The expenses of viewing and assessing damages, and all other incidental matters, not fully provided for in *Expenses of viewing, &c.*

this act, shall be governed by the general road laws of the commonwealth

Approved April 27th, 1870, P. L. 1283.

AN ACT to repeal an act, entitled "An Act authorizing the burgess and council of the borough of Sunbury, in Northumberland county, to open and extend Second and Fourth streets, in said borough," approved the twenty-second day of April, Anno Domini one thousand eight hundred and seventy.

Authority to open and extend Second and Fourth streets,repealed

SEC. 1. *Be it enacted &c.*, That the act approved the twenty-second day of April, Anno Domino one thousand eight hundred and seventy, entitled "An Act authorizing the burgess and council of the borough of Sunbury, in Northumberland county, to open and extend Second street and Fourth street, in said borough," be and the same is hereby repealed.

Streets laid out but not opened, vacated.

SEC. 2. That any street, or streets, laid out or extended under the provisions of the said act, and not already opened and used, be and the same is hereby vacated.

Approved May 19th 1871, P. L. 951.

AN ACT authorizing the burgess and town council of the borough of Sunbury to erect a lock-up.

Borough authorities may provide lock-up

SEC. 1 *Be it enacted, &c.*, That the burgess and town council of the borough of Sunbury, in the county of Northumberland, be and they are hereby authorized and empowered to build or otherwise provide within the said borough, a suitable building for the security and temporary detention of any person or persons committed by a justice of the peace or burgess of the said borough, for any violation of the laws of this commonwealth, or of any ordinance of the said borough, or upon the arrest of a peace officer or police in the absence of such justice of the peace, for which such person or persons could be lawfully committed to the common jail of said county : *Provided*, That no person shall be confined in said lock-up house at any time for a longer period than seventy-two hours, except such person or persons be charged with an indictable offense, and it be necessary to detain such person or persons for legal examination. — Confinement in lock-up limited

SEC. 2. That all fees for arrest, commitment and safe-keeping of any person shall be taxed by any justice of the peace or burgess, and paid by the prosecutor or defendant or borough of Sunbury, as the issues of the case on which such defendant or defendants shall be committed, may be determined and required. — Payment of fees

SEC. 3. That the burgess and town council of said borough, or a majority of them, may appropriate and pay for the erection of said lock-up house and lot of ground, such sum of money, out of the funds of said borough, as they deem necessary : *Provided however*, That the cost of such lock-up house and lot shall not exceed one thousand dollars. — May appropriate borough funds for lock-up. Cost limited.

Approved May 25th, 1871, P. L. 1153.

— — —

AN ACT fixing the place for holding elections in the East ward.

SEC. 1. *Be it enacted, &c.*, That the place for holding all general, special and borough elections in the East ward of the borough of Sunbury, in the county of Northumberland, shall be held hereafter at the public house of Edward T. Drumheller, in said ward.

Approved December 27th, 1871, P. L. 1872, 1392.

A SUPPLEMENT to an act, entitled "An Act to erect the town of Sunbury, in the county of Northumberland, into a borough," approved the twenty-fourth day of March, Anno Domini one thousand seven hundred and ninety-seven, authorizing the said borough of Sunbury to make regulations respecting markets, and market days, and weights and measures therein.

Council may make market regulations.

SEC. 1. *Be it enacted, &c.*, That it shall be lawful for the burgesses, assistant burgesses and common councilmen of the borough of Sunbury, in the county of Northumberland, in common council assembled, to make all needful regulations respecting markets and market days, hawking and peddling of market produce and other articles in the said borough, and for the inspection and measurement or weight of cord-wood, hay, coal and other articles, sold or offered for sale in said borogh, and to regulate the scales, weights and measures within the said borough, according to the standard of the commonwealth.

Approved April 2rd, 1872, P. L. 860.

———

AN ACT to authorize the town council of the borough of Sunbury to borrow money.

May borrow money and issue bonds.

SEC. 1. *Be it enacted, &c.*, That for the purpose of funding and consolidating the whole outstanding debt of the borough of Sunbury, of whatever nature it may be, the town council of said borough or their successors, are hereby authorized and empowered to borrow any sum or sums, not exceeding in the aggregate thirty-five thousand dollars, and may issue coupon bonds therefor in the corporate name of the borough, payable ten years after date, with seven per centum interest, payable semi-annually ; said coupon to be receivable at par in payment of all taxes laid by said

Exempt from borough tax.

town council ; said bond shall not be taxable for borough

purposes, and shall be signed by the chief burgess, sealed with the borough seal and attested by the town clerk.

SEC. 2. That all former acts or parts of acts, authorizing the town council of the borough of Sunbury to borrow money, be and the same is hereby repealed. **Repeal.**

Approved January 31st, 1873, P. L. 106.

PROVISIONS OF THE STATE CONSTITUTION SPECIALLY RELATING TO BOROUGHS.

ARTICLE III.
Legislation.

SECTION 7. The General Assembly shall not pass any local or special law. * * * * **Limitations on special legislation, &c.**

Regulating the affairs of * * wards and boroughs: * *

Authorizing the laying out, opening, altering or maintaining, roads, highways, streets or alleys: * * *

Vacating roads, town plats, streets or alleys: * * *

Relating to cemeteries, graveyards, public grounds not of the State: * * *

Incorporating cities, towns or vilages, or changing their charters: * * *

Changing * * borough limits: * * *

Creating offices, or prescribing the powers and duties of officers * * in boroughs:

SEC. 13. No law shall extend the term of any public officer, or increase or diminish his salary or emoluments, after his election or appointment.

ARTICLE VIII.
Suffrage and Elections.

SECTION 1. Every male citizen twenty-one years of age possessing the following qualifications, shall be entitled to vote at all elections. * * * **Qualifications of voters.**

*Third—*He shall have resided in the election district where he shall offer to vote at least two months immediately preceeding the election.

Municipal elections. Sec. 3. All elections for * * ward and borough * * officers, for regular terms of service, shall be held on the third Tuesday of February.

Representatives to vote *viva voce* Sec. 12. All elections by persons in a representive capacity shall be *viva voce.*

ARTICLE IX.
Taxation and Finance.

Taxes to be uniform. Section 1. All taxes shall be uniform, upon the same class of subject, within the the territorial limits of the authority levying the tax and shall be levied and collected **Exemptions.** under general laws ; but the General Assembly may, by general laws, exempt from taxation public property used for public purposes, actual places of religious worship, places of burial not used or held for private or corporate profit, and institutions of purely public charity.

Limitation of power to exempt Sec. 2. All laws exempting property from taxation, other than the property above enumerated, shall be void.

Municipalities not to become stockholders,&c Sec. 7. The General Assembly shall not authorize any * * borough * * to become a stockholder in any company,association or corporation,or to obtain or appropriate money for it, or to loan its credit to, any corporation, association, institution or individual.

Municipal debts limited. Sec. 8. The debt of any * * borough, * * except as herein provided, shall never exceed seven per centum upon the assessed value of the taxable property therein, nor shall any such municipality or district incur any new debt, or increase its indebtedness to an amount exceeding two per centum upon such assessed valuation of property, without the assent of the electors thereof at a public election in such manner as shall be provided by law. * * *

Re-payment of municipal debt to be provided for. Sec. 10. Any * * municipality incuring any indebtedness shall, at or before the time of so doing, provide for the collection of an annual tax sufficient to pay the interest and also the principal thereof within thirty years.

ARTICLE XVI.
Private Corporations.

SECTION 8. Municipal and other corporations and individuals invested with the privilege of taking private property for public use shall make just compensation for property taken, injured or destroyed by the construction or enlargement of their works highways or improvements, which compensation shall be paid or secured before such taking injury or destruction. The General Assembly is hereby prohibited from depriving any person of an appeal from any preliminary assessment of damages against any such corporations or individuals made by viewers or otherwise; and the amount of such damages as in all cases of appeal shall on the demand of either party be determined by a jury according to the course of the common law.

The taking and injury of private property to be compensated

Appeal from assessment of damages.

ARTICLE XVII.
Railroads and Canals.

SECTION 9. No street passenger railway shall be constructed within the limits of any * * borough, * * without the consent of its local authorities.

Passenger railroads not to be constructed without theconsent of municipal authorities.

GENERAL LAWS APPLICABLE TO THE AFFAIRS OF THE BOROUGH OF SUNBURY.

I. DIVISION OF WARDS AND EXTENSION OF LIMITS.

1. Erection of new wards.
2. Parts of wards may be consolidated.
3. Commissioners to be appointed.
4. Proceedings on report. Review.
5. Councilmen and school directors.
6. Compensation of viewers.
7. Increase of councilmen and school directors.
8. Each ward to be an election district. Officers to be elected.
9. Duties of assessors.
10. Returns of elections.
11. How vacancies filled.
12. Court may fix places of election.
13. How limits may be changed.
14. Application for annexation.
15. Proceedings thereon.

1. The several courts of quarter sessions shall have authority, within their respective counties, to divide boroughs

14 May 1874 § 1. P. L 159.

48

Erection of wards. into wards, to erect new wards out of parts of two or more adjoining wards, to divide any ward already erected into two or more wards, to alter the lines of any two or more adjoining wards, so as to suit the convenience of the inhabitants thereof, and to cause the lines or boundaries to be ascertained.

2. The several courts of quarter sessions shall have authority within their respective counties to divide boroughs into wards, by erecting two or more wards or parts of two or more wards into one ward, so as to suit the convenience of the inhabitants thereof.

24 March 77 §1. P. L 47.
Consolidation of parts of wards.

14 May 1874 § 2 P. L. 159.
Commissioners to be appointed 3. Upon application by petition of at least twenty freeholders, resident of the borough or ward, to a court of quarter sessions, for the purpose of dividing any borough into wards or erecting one or more new wards out of parts of two or more adjoining wards, of dividing any ward already erected into two or more wards, of altering the lines of any wards, or of ascertaining and establishing the lines or boundaries of any ward or wards, the said court shall appoint three impartial men to inquire into the propriety of granting the Their duties. prayer of the petition; and it shall be the duty of the commissioners so appointed, or any two of them, to make a plot or draft of the borough or wards proposed to be divided, of the proposed new wards and the division lines proposed to be made thereon, or of the lines proposed to be altered of two or more adjoining wards, or of the lines proposed to be ascertained and established, as the case may be, if the same cannot be fully designated by natural lines or boundaries; all which they or any two of them shall report to the next court of quarter sessions, together with their opinion of the same.

4. When a report has been made by said commissioners Ibid, § 3.
Proceedings on report. it shall be confirmed *nisi* by said court, which confirmation shall become absolute, unless exceptions be filed to the same, not later than the third day of next term of said court; and should exceptions be filed, as aforesaid, they shall be

disposed of on evidence, as said court shall deem just: *Provided*, That if desired, a review may be had if, in the opinion of the court it may be necessary to secure a fair Review. adjudication of the same; said review to be asked for before the report has been confirmed absolutely, however.

5. When said report shall have been confirmed by the 16 Feb 1883 § 1 P. L. 5. court, it shall at the same time decree the election of an Court to decree election of councilmen. equal number of councilmen in each of the wards, in such a manner as not to interfere with the terms of those heretofore elected. From and after such division into wards, or where any such division has heretofore been made, each ward shall elect, from among the residents of said ward, not Each ward to elect school-directors. less than one nor more than three school directors, as shall be determined by the court of quarter sessions, of the said Court to fix the number. county decreeing such division; and it is hereby made the duty of the burgess and town clerk, of said borough, or Duty of burgess and town clerk. either of them, at least thirty days before election, to present, under oath, a petition to the said court or the president judge thereof, setting forth the names of the present directors, and their ward residences: *Provided*, That at the election to be held on the third Tuesday of February, one thousand eight hundred and eighty-three, the petition herein required shall be at least five days before said election. Until such time as the terms of office, of all the pres- Vacancies, how filled. ent school directors in said borough, shall have expired, the vacancies, as they occur, shall be filled by electing a person or persons, from the ward or wards, then unrepresented in Court to indicate wards. said school board, to be indicated by the court of quarter sessions of the county, or the president judge thereof if the court is not in session.

6. The compensation of the commissioners shall be the 14 May 1874 § 5 P. L. 159. same as now paid to road viewers, and to be paid in the Compensation. same manner.

7. Upon the division of any borough into wards, or the 17 Feb. 1876 § 1 P. L. 6. erection of a new ward or wards in any borough, being had pursuant to the provisions of an act of the general assembly,

Increase of councilmen and school directors. entitled "an act to prescribe the manner by which courts may divide boroughs into wards," approved the 14th day of May, Anno Domini, 1874, it shall be lawful for the court decreeing such division, in all cases where the number of councilmen or school directors of such borough cannot be equally divided among the respective wards created by such division, to increase the number of councilmen and school directors to and not exceeding such number as will enable the court to make an equal apportionment of the same among the respective wards.

10 May 1878 § 1.
P. L 51.

On division of boroughs, each ward to be a seperate election district. 8. Whenever any borough in this commonwealth may be divided into wards, in accordance with the provisions of the act to which this is a supplement, every such ward from and after such division shall be a separate election district, and annually thereafter shall elect not less than one nor more than three members of the borough councils, and shall select such other public officers as are authorized in borough, wards and election districts under existing laws : Election of officers
a. *Provided however*, That in every such borough there shall be elected a burgess, assistant burgess, two justices of the peace, three auditors, high constable, who shall be chosen by the concurrent votes of each ward, and their election shall be ascertained and declared by the joint certificates of the judges of elections as hereinafter provided : *And provided further*, That officers who shall be chosen by the concurrent votes of said wards, shall be chosen for such terms as are now provided by existing laws.

Ibid, § 2.

Duties of assessors. 9. In all boroughs which may be divided into more than two wards under said act, the assessors elected for the various wards shall jointly perform the duties required by law of assistant assessors in making the triennial assessment in the several wards, and there shall not in any such wards be an assistant assessor elected.

Ibid § 3.

Returns of election. 10. On the first Friday after each borough election held in boroughs divided as aforesaid, the judges of election of the various wards in such boroughs shall meet at the

a. See supra 5.

place of meeting of town councils in such borough, at nine
o'clock in the forenoon, and after organizing shall canvass
the vote cast for officers required by the first section of this
act to be elected by the concurrent votes of the various
wards in such borough, and shall ascertain and declare the
result of such election and grant certificates to the persons
elected to fill such offices.

11. Such borough officers as may be in office at the
time of the division of any such borough into wards as
aforesaid, shall remain in office until the expiration of the
terms for which they may have been elected; and in case
any vacancy shall occur, the same may be filled by appointment of the court of quarter sessions of the proper county
until the next regular borough election.

12. The court of quarter sessions of the proper county
shall have power to fix the place of holding elections in the
various wards of every such borough, and from time to
time, as occasion may require, to change the same in the
manner prescribed by existing laws, and shall appoint for
each ward such judges and inspectors of election to hold
the first election after such division as are by law required
in the case of borough and township elections.

13. The several courts of quarter sessions within this
commonwealth, by and with the concurrence of the grand
jury of the county, shall have power to change the limits
of any authorized borough within this commonwealth.

14. When an application is made to the court by the inhabitants of any lots, outlots or other tracts of land, adjacent to a borough, to be annexed to said borough it shall
be in writing, and shall be signed by a majority of the
freeholders residing within the limits to be annexed, and
shall set forth a particular description of the boundaries,
exhibiting the courses and distances in words at length,
and be accompanied with a plot or draft of the same; it
shall also appear by proof satisfactory to court, that a notice of the intended application has been personally served

Ibid § 4.

Persons in office
at time of divi-
sion to remain.

Vacancies.

Ibid, § 5.

Court may fix
place of election

And appoint of-
ficers.

17 May 1883 § 1
P. L. 36.

Power to alter
borough limits.

11 June 79 § 1.
P. L. 150.

Applications for
annexation of
adjacent lands.

upon the burgess and town council of the borough and the supervisors of the township in which the petitioners then reside, and that public notice has been given of such application in at least one newspaper of the proper county, by publication for a period of not less than thirty days immediately before the petition shall be presented.

Ibid, § 3.
Proceedings on application.

15. The court shall cause the aforesaid application to be laid before the grand jury when in session. and if a majority of said grand jury, after a full investigation of the case, shall find that the conditions prescribed by this act have been complied with, and shall believe that it is expedient to grant the prayer of the petitioners, they shall certify the same to the court, which certificate shall be entered of record and may be confirmed by the court; and if the decree of the court shall be in conformity with the prayer of the petitioners, the said petition and decree shall be recorded in the recorder's office of the proper county, at the expense of the applicants, and from thenceforth the said limits so annexed, shall be deemed, taken and allowed to be a part of said borough, and subject to the jurisdiction and government of the municipal authorities of said borough, as fully as if the same had been originally a part thereof; but if the court shall deem further investigation necessary, they may take such order thereon as to right and justice shall appertain.

II. CORPORATE POWERS.

16. Power to license theatres, &c.
17. How enforced.
18. Damages for change of grade.

Viewers to be appointed, &c.
19. Regulation of wooden. buildings.

5 May 1876 § 1.
P. L. 112.
Power to license theatres, &c.

16. Every borough or incorporated town heretofore incorporated, or hereafter to be incorporated, within this commonwealth, shall, in addition to the powers already granted or to be granted, have the right and authority to regulate, license or prohibit theatrical exhibitions, concerts, circuses, shows, mountebanks and jugglers, and all other exhibitions, within the limits of said boroughs or incorporated towns.

17. For the purpose of carrying this act into effect, every Ibid, §3.
borough or incorporated town within this commonwealth How enforced.
shall have power, by its proper officers, to pass such ordinances or by-laws as may be necessary for that purpose, and
also to impose fines, to be collected by an action of debt, or
penalties, to be inforced by summary conviction, as for a
breach of the peace, before any alderman, magistrate or
justice of the peace of said boroughs or incorporated towns.

18. In all cases where the proper authorities of any bor- 24 March 1878 §1 P. L 129.
ough, within this commonwealth, have or may hereafter
change the grade or lines of any street or alley, or in any Damages for change of grade
way alter or enlarge the same, thereby causing damage to
the owner or owners of property abutting thereon, without
consent of such owner, or in case they fail to agree with the
owner thereof for the proper compensation for the damages
so done, or likely to be done, or sustained, by reason there-
of, or by reason of the legal incapacity of such owner, no Viewers to be appointed.
such compensation can be agreed upon, the court of com-
mon pleas of the proper county, on application thereto by
petition, either by the burgess and councilmen of said borough or the owner of the property for which damage is
claimed, or any one on behalf of either, shall appoint five
disinterested citizens of such county neither of whom shall
be owners of property on said street, who shall meet upon
the premises, at a time by them appointed, of which they
shall give ten days' notice by handbills posted up on such
street in the vicinity of the premises; and the said viewers,
or any three of them, having been first duly sworn or af-
firmed to perform their duties justly and impartially and Their duties.
a true report make, shall view the said street or alley, and
premises affected by the change or enlargement thereof,
having due regard to and making just allowance for advantages which may have resulted, or which may seem likely
to result, to the owner or owners of property abutting
thereon, for which damages may be allowed or claimed
and after such comparison shall estimate and determine

whether any, and if any, how much damage such property owner may have sustained, or seems likely to sustain, by

Report.

reason thereof, and make report of the same to the next
term of said court, and if no exceptions be filed within ten

Compensation.

days thereafter, the court shall confirm the same and enter
judgment thereon with costs, each viewer to be entitled
to receive one dollar and fifty cents per day, from which

Appeal.

judgment either party shall be entitled to an appeal as in
other cases.

**3 June 1885 § 1.
P. L. 55.**

**Councils auth-
orized to regu-
late, by ordin-
ance the erec-
tion of wooden
buildings in
boroughs.**

19. The town council of all boroughs now incorporated
in the commonwealth or that may be hereafter incorpora-
ed, are hereby authorized and empowered to pass such
ordinances as may be necessary to regulate or prevent the
erection of any wooden dwelling-house, shop, warehouse,
stores, carriage house, stable, or other frame tenement with-
the limits of the respective boroughs.

III. Indebtness and Loans.

**20 April 1874 § 1
P L. 65.**

**Indebtedness
not to exceed
seven per cent
of the assessed
valuation.**

Penalty.

20. Whenever the debt of any borough, within this commonwealth shall be equal to seven per centum upon the
assessed value of the taxable property, as fixed by the last
preceeding assessed valuation therein, it shall be unlawful
to increase the same, and all such increase shall be void, and
any obligation issued for such increase, or any part thereof,
shall be of no binding force upon such municipality or district ; and each of the officers thereof wilfully authorizing
such increase, or executing any obligation therefor, shall be
guilty of a misdemeanor, and upon conviction thereof, shall

be fined not exceeding ten thousand dollars, and undergo an imprisonment not exceeding one year, or either, at the discretion of the court trying the same.

20 April 1874.

21. Any borough may incur debt, or increase its indebtedness to an amount in the aggregate not exceeding two per centum upon the assessed value of the taxable property therein, as fixed and determined by the last preceding assessed valuation thereof, and the corporate authorities of such municipality may, by a vote thereof, duly recorded upon its minutes, authorize and direct the incurring or the increase of such debt to the amount aforesaid, and may issue coupon bonds or other securities therefor, in sums not less than one hundred dollars each, bearing interest at a rate not exceeding six per centum per annum, payable semi-annually, and the principal thereof reimbursable at a period not exceeding thirty years from the date at which the same is authorized. And an annual tax, commencing the first year after such debt shall be increased or incurred, equal to at least eight per centum of the amount thereof, shall be forthwith assessed, to provide for the payment of the interest and the liquidation of the principal thereof; and the moneys arising from such tax shall be applied annually, and as fast as the same accumulates, to the redemption at par of the said outstanding obligations.

Ibid, § 2.
Debts equal to two per cent, on the valuation may be incurred.
Bonds to be issued therefor.
When principal to be payable.
Annual tax to be levied.
Application thereof.

22. Before issuing any such obligation or security, it shall be the duty of the principal officer or officers of such municipality or incorporated district, to prepare a statement, showing the actual indebtedness of such district, the amount of the last preceding assessed valuation of the taxable property therein, the amount of debt to be incurred, the form, number and date of maturity of the obligations to be issued therefor, and the amount of the annual tax levied and assessed to pay the said indebtedness, and he shall make and append thereto his oath or affirmation of the truth of the facts therein stated, and shall file the said statement in the office of the clerk of the court of quarter sessions of the

Officers to prepare and file certain statements.
Penalty for neglect.

Copies to be evidence. proper county ; upon failure so to do, he shall be guilty of a misdemeanor, and on conviction thereof, shall be punished as provided in the first section of this act. Certified copies of the record of such statement, under the seal of said court, shall be competent evidence in all the courts of this com-
Sale of bonds. monwealth : *Provided,* That the bonds shall not be sold at less than their par value.

Ibid § 3. 23. The indebtedness of any county, city borough, town-
Vote of electors on increase of indebtedness. ship, school district or other municipality or incorporated district, in this commonwealth, may be authorized to be increased to an amount exceeding two per centum, and not exceeding seven per centum, upon the last preceeding assessed valuation of the taxable property therein, with the assent of the electors thereof, duly obtained at a public election to be held in the said district or municipality.
Notice to be given. Whenever the corporate authorities of any county, city, borough, township, school district or other municipality or incorporated district, by their ordinance or vote, shall have signified a desire to make such increase of indebtedness, they shall give notice, during at least thirty days, by weekly advertisements in the newspapers, not exceeding three in said district ; and if no newspaper be published therein, by at least twenty printed handbills posted in the most public parts thereof, of an election to be held at the place or places of holding the municipal elections in said district or municipality, on a day to be by them fixed, for the purpose of obtaining the assent of the electors thereof to such increase
Form of notice. of indebtedness ; said notice shall contain a statement of the amount of the existing debt, of the amount and percentage of the proposed increase, and of the purposes for which the indebtedness is to be increased.

When election to be held. 24. Such election shall be held at the places and by the officers provided by law for the holding of municipal elec-
Mode of conducting elections. tions ; and it shall be the duty of the inspectors and judges of such elections to receive tickets, either written or printed, from electors qualified under the constitution of this

state to vote in such district, labeled on the outside, "increase of debt," and containing in the inside the words, "no increase of debt," or "debt may be increasd," and to deposit said tickets in a box provided for that purpose, as is provided by law in regard to other tickets received at said election; and the tickets so received shall be counted, and a return thereof made to the clerk of the court of quarter sessions of the proper county, duly certified, as is required by law, together with a certified copy of the ordinance and the advertisement; and the said clerk shall make a record of the same, and furnish a certified copy thereof, under seal, showing the result, to the corporate authorities of such municipality, and the same shall be placed of record upon the minutes thereof. The corporate authorities of such municipality shall, in all cases, fix the time of holding such election on the day of the municipal or of the general election, unless more than ninety days elapse between the date of the ordinance or vote desiring such increase, and the day of holding the said municipal or general election; if any other day be fixed for such election, the expense of holding the same shall be paid by the municipality for the benefit of which it is held. In receiving and counting, and in making returns of the votes cast, the inspectors, judges and clerks of said election shall be governed by the laws of this commonwealth regulating municipal elections; and all the penalties of the said election laws, for the violation thereof, are hereby extended to, and shall apply to the voters, inspectors, judges and clerks voting at and in attendance upon the elections held under the provisions of this act.

Returns.

To be recorded

When election to be held.

Expenses.

General election laws to be applicable.

25. Whenever, by returns of such election, it shall appear that there is a majority voting for "no increase of debt," such increase shall not be made, nor shall any other election upon the same subject to be held in that municipality, for one year from the date of such preceding election. If the return of such election shall show a majority voting that "debt may be increased," the corporate authorities of the municipality may increese the same to the amount named

Ibid § 4.

On majority against inrease, no other election to be held for one year.

How increase to be made on affirmative vote.

58

and specified in the notice given by them for holding of such election, in the manner and subject to all of the requirements provided by the second section of this act, for increasing indebtedness to an amount not exceeding two per centum, including the sworn statement, to be filed in the office of the clerk of the court of quarter sessions of the proper county , and they shall, before issuing any obligation therefor, assess and levy an annual tax, the collection whereof shall commence the first year after the said increase, which tax shall be equal to at least eight per centum of the amount of such increased debt, and which shall be sufficient for and be applied exclusively to the payment of the interest and the principal of such debt, within a period not exceeding thirty years from the date of such increase ; and the moneys arising from such tax shall be applied annually, and as fast as the same accumulates, to the redemption at par of the said outstanding obligations.

Annual tax to be levied.

20 April 1674 § 5

Indebtedness defined.

26. The word "indebtedness," used in this act, shall be deemed, held and taken to include all and all manner of debt, as well floating as funded, of the said municipality ; and the net amount of such indebtedness shall be ascertained by deducting from the gross amount thereof, the moneys in the treasury,all outstanding solvent debts,and all revenues applicable, within one year, to the payment of the same.

12 April 1875 § 1 P. L 46.

Publication of annual statements

27. The corporate authority of every such municipality or district shall, at the end of their fiscal year, prepare and publish in at least two newspapers of said municipality or of the county in which the same is situate, if so many be printed therein, a statement showing in detail, the actual indebtedness, the amount of the funded debt, the amount of the floating debt thereof, the valuation of taxable property therein, the assets of the corporation, with the character and value thereof, and the date of the maturity of the respective forms of funded debt thereof ; and a neglect or failure so to do shall be a misdemeanor,punishable by fine not exceeding one thousand dollars.

28. The existing indebtedness of any such municipality evidenced by outstanding bonds or certificates of indebtedness heretofore issued, may be provided for as the same shall mature, by a reissue of bonds or certificates of indebtedness to the holders of the said outstanding bonds or certificates, or by the issue and sale, at not less than par, of new bonds or certificates; and the present floating indebtedness of any such municipality may be funded by the issue and sale, at not less than par, of bonds or certificates of indebtedness, in sums not less than one hundred dollars each: *Provided*, That no such bond or certificate shall be issued for a longer period than thirty years from the date thereof. And it shall be the duty of the proper corporate authorities of such municipality to provide for the payment ment of principal and interest of all such bonds, in the manner pointed out in the fourth section of this act.

Ibid, § 7.
Reissues of bonds for existing indebtedness.
Funding floating debt.

29. In all cases where any borough in this commonwealth has, by virtue of any general or special act of assembly, issued bonds, either with or without coupons attached, to secure any indebtedness of any such borough, it shall be lawful for the burgess and town council of any such borough to redeem any or all of the bonds so issued as aforesaid, before the maturity thereof, with the consent of the holders thereof, and issue new bonds to secure such indebtedness, at any lower rate of interest; the bonds so issued not to exceed in amount the amount of the bonds so redeemed.

11 June 1879 §1.
P. L. 153.
Redemption of bonds before maturity, authorized.
New bonds, may be issued.

30. In all cases where any county, city (except cities of the first and second classes), boroughs, municipality or school district in this commonwealth, has, by virtue of any general or special act of assembly, issued bonds or other interest bearing evidences of indebtedness, with or without interest coupons attached, to secure any indebtedness of any such county, city, borough, municipality or school district, it shall be lawful for any such county, city (except cities of the first and second classes), borough, municipality or school district, to redeem or pay off any or all of the bonds or other inter-

74 April 1881, § 1
P. L. 14.
When bonds may be paid off

est bearing evidences of indebtedness so issued, which may
be matured or payable, or whenever any county, city (except cities of the first and second classes), borough, muni-

Issue of new bonds. cipality or school district shall have the option to redeem
or pay any such bonds or interest bearing evidences of in-

Rate of Interest debtedness, and for that purpose shall have the right to issue and sell bonds, either with or without coupons attached,

When redeemable. bearing interest not exceeding six per centum per annum,

Limit of issue. redeemable at the option of the county, city, borough, municipality or school district, issuing the same, in five years,

Exemption from local taxation. payable at any time not exceeding twenty years after the
date thereof, and not exceeding in aggregate the amount of
the bonds or other evidences of indebtedness so redeemed or
paid, and the said bonds so issued or sold, in accordance
with the provisions of this act, shall be exempt from taxation, except for state purposes.

Ibid 2.

Holders of old bonds to first have the right to exchange for new bonds. 31. The holders of any bonds or evidences of indebtedness as aforesaid, which may be matured or payable or
which may be payable or redeemable at the option of any
county, city (except cities of the first and second classes),
borough, municipality or school district, but which may
not be matured or payable, shall first have the right to
surrender said bonds and receive bonds, issued under the
provisions of this act, in like amount in lieu thereof, and
notice shall be given of the right of the holder of such
bonds in surrender the same and accept bonds issued under

Notices to be given to such holders. this act, by publication for three weeks, in at least one
newspaper published in the county, and in case of a city,
borough, municipality or school district, by like publication in at least one newspaper published in the county, in
which the said borough, municipality or school district,
may be located, before any bonds shall be sold under the
first section of this act.

23 March 1877 P. L. 20

Taxpayers may inquire into validity of judgments. 32. In case of any unsatisfied judgment or any suit or
process of law against any township, borough, school or
poor district, or other municipal district, in this commonwealth, any tax payer of said district may inquire into the

validity of any judgment or defend said district in any suit
or judgment, upon petition, accompanied by affidavit that
said taxpayer believes that injustice will be done to said
district in said suit or judgment, presented to the court of
common pleas in which said suit may be pending or judgment may exist, shall have the right to come into court and
defend said district in any suit, and inquire into the validi- *Or defend districts in suits.*
ty of any judgment against said municipal district, as fully
and completely as the officers of said district would by law
have the right to do: *Provided*, That said tax payer shall,
whenever the court shall deem it necessary, file in said *To file bond if required by court.*
court of common pleas a bond, with one or more sufficient
surities to be approved of by the said court, to indemnify
and save harmless said district from all costs that may accrue in said suit subsequently to filing said petition.

IV. ELECTIONS AND TERMS OF OFFICE.

33. That upon the petition of the councils of any bor- *24 March 1877;1 P. L. 36*
ough heretofore incorporated or hereafter to be incorpora- *Vacancies, how filled.*
ed within this commonwealth to the court of quarter sess- *(i.)*
ions of the proper county, representing that any vacancy
or vacancies in their own body or in any other borough
officers exists, said court shall have the right and authority to fill such vacancy by appointment, said appointees to
hold office until the succeeding municipal election: *Provided*, That this act shall not be construed to change the
manner of filling any such vacancy in any borough where
such authority now exists by general or special law.

34. That it shall be lawful for the qualified voters of the *1 June 1883 § 2 P. L. 54.*
boroughs in the Commonwealth of Pennsylvania, not now *Time and manner of electing town council in*
enjoying this right by special statues, at the first election

a. See *Infra* 36 as to Councilmen.

certain bor-
oughs. for borough officers, next ensuing the passage of this act to
elect one-third of the whole number of councilmen to serve
for one year, one-third to serve for two-years, and one-third
for three years, and annually thereafter to elect one-third

In boroughs
where chief
burgess is one of
six members. of the whole number to serve for three years: *Provided*,
That in boroughs in which the chief burgess is one of six
members of town council, the chief burgess shall be elected
annually, and at the first election held for borough officers
two of the councilmen shall be elected for one year, three
for two years, and at succeeding elections two or three, al-
ternately, for a term of two years.

Ibid § 3. 35. It shall be lawful for the qualified voters of the bor-
In boroughs
having even
number not di-
visible by three oughs of the Commonwealth of Pennsylvania, which have
an even number of councilmen not devisible by three, and
which do not now enjoy the right by special statutes, at the
first election for borough officers next ensuing the passage
of this act, to elect one-half the whole number of councilmen for one year, one-half for two years, and annually
thereafter to elect one-half of the whole number for two
years: *Provided* That at the first election for borough
officers, held after the passage of this act, the voters shall
Terms to be
stated ou bal-
lots. put on their ballots the names of those who are to be elected
for the different terms.

Ibid, § 4. 36. The members of town council shall have power to
Vacancies, how
filled. fill any vacancy which may occur therein by death, resignation, removal from the borough, or otherwise, until the
next annual election for members of town council, when
such vacancy shall be filled by electing a qualified citizen
to supply the same, for the balance of the unexpired term.

4 June, 1883 § 1
P. L. 66. 37. On the third Tuesday of February, Anno Domini
one thousand eight hundred and eighty-two, the qualified
Each borough
and township to
elect overseers
of the poor. voters of each borough and township within this Commonwealth, shall elect two persons overseers of the poor, the
one receiving the highest number of votes to hold his office
for the term of two years, and the one receiving the next
Term of office
regulated. highest number of votes to hold his office for the term of
one year, and annually thereafter they shall elect one per-

son overseer of the poor, to hold his office for the term of two years. 13 June 1883 § 1
P. L. 121.

38. The term of office of every borough officer hereafter elected, whose term of office would under existing laws, expire on the first Monday of April, of any year, shall expire ^a on the first Monday of March next preceding said first Monday of April, and the terms of the successors of such borough officers shall begin on the first Monday of March, and shall continue for the period now fixed for the duration thereof by existing laws. First Monday of
March fixed as
commencement
of term of office

V. BOROUGH AUDITORS.

39. When to meet.
40. To publish annual statements.

41. Penalty for neglecting.

39. The borough auditors shall meet on the second Monday of March of the year one thousand eight hundred and eighty-three and on the second Monday of March in each year thereafter, for the settlement of all accounts by them to be settled, except the accounts of the school directors and school treasurer. 13 June 1883 §2
P. L. 121.

Auditor to meet
and settle all
accounts on the
second Monday
of March.

40. The auditors of the several townships and boroughs within this commonwealth are hereby authorized and required to publish, by posting handbills, either printed or written, in at least five public places within their respective townships or boroughs, and itemized annual statement of the receipts and expenditures of the borough councils, road commissioners, supervisors, overseers of the poor and school directors, for the year preceeding the annual settlement for their respective districts; said handbills to be posted within ten days after such settlement; and further, it shall be the duty of said auditors to file a copy of the same with the town clerk in the respective districts, and 21 April 1874 §2
P. L. 112.

To publish an-
nual statements

Copy to be filed.

---

a. The act of 10th March, 1875, P. L. 6, fixed the first Monday of April for commencement of terms of office of all borough officers, and the organization of council, this provision being inconsistant with the present act, council now organize on the first Monday in March.

also with the clerk of the court of quarter sessions, which shall be at all times subject to inspection by any citizen thereof : *Provided*, That where any two of said offices shall be exercised by the same persons only one statement shall be required : *Also provided*, That nothing in this act shall be construed to interfere with the present law which requires annual statements of the receipts and expenditures of the borough councils, road commissioners, supervisors, overseers of the poor and school directors to be advertised in all the weekly newspapers published in the respective localities.

Ibid § 3

Penalty for violation of the act

41. In case of neglect or refusal to comply with the provisions of this act, the auditors so neglecting or refusing shall each pay a penalty of twenty dollars, to be recovered in the same manner as debts of similar amount are by law recoverable, by suit instituted in the name of the school district, upon the complaint of any tax-paying citizen of of the same, and the proceeds thereof to be paid into the schoool treasury of said district.

VI. TAXES AND TAX COLLECTORS.

42. Tax collector to be elected annually.
43. Court to fill vacancies therein.
44. Bonds, etc.
45. Duplicate to issue before August first.
46. Powers and liabilities of collectors.
47. Books to be open to inspection.
48. Reduction for prompt payment and penalty on delayed payment.
49. Time and place for receipt of tax.
50. Compensation.
51. Exonerations.
52. Settlement of accounts.
53. Repealing clause.

25 June 1885 § 1 P. L. 187.

Borough and township tax collectors to be annually elected in February.

Term of office.

42. The qualified electors of each borough and township in this Commonwealth shall, on the third Tuesday of February of each year hereafter, elect an officer, to be styled collector of taxes, whose term of office shall commence on the first Monday of April next after his election.

Ibid § 2

Vacancies to be filled by court of quarter sessions.

43. The courts of quarter sessions shall have power to fill, by appointment, all vacancies in the said office, within their respective counties. And, if any person elected to fill said office shall fail to give bond and qualify as hereinafter pro-

vided, on or before the fourth day of the term of said court
next ensuing his election, the said court shall declare his
office vacant and appoint a suitable person, resident in the
proper borough or township, to fill the same.

44. The collector of taxes shall, before he enters upon the
duties of his office, take and subscribe an oath of office, and
file the same in the office of the court of quarter sessions of
the proper county, and shall also enter into a bond to the
Commonwealth, in double the probable amount of taxes
that will come into his hands, with at least two sufficient
sureties ; said bond to be approved by said court or a judge
thereof in vacation, and filed in the office of the clerk of the
said court; the condition of which bond shall be, that the
said collector shall well and truly collect and pay over or
account for, according to law, the whole amount of taxes
charged and assessed in the duplicates, which shall be delivered to him.

45. The several county, borough, township, school, poor
and other authorities now empowered, and which may
hereafter be empowered, to levy taxes within the several
boroughs and townships of this Commonwealth, shall, on
or before the first day of August of each year after the first
election of collector of taxes under this act, issue their respective duplicates of taxes assessed to the collector of taxes
of their respective boroughs and townships with their war-
rants attached, directing and authorizing him to collect the
same, but road taxes may be worked out as heretofore:
Provided, That such special and other road taxes, as it may
be lawful and necessary to collect in money, may, at the
discretion of the supervisors or road commissioners, be
placed in the hands of the collector of taxes, with their
warrant for collection by him; for which he shall receive
five per centum of the amount collected by him, or the same
may be collected by the supervisors or road commissioners
as heretofore. *Provided further*, That the limitations in this
act, as to time and the requirements hereof relating to

Ibid § 3
Oath to be tak-
en and filed.

Bond, with sure-
ties, to be given

And approved
by the court
and filed.
Condition of
bond.

Ibid § 4
Duplicates to be
issued on or be-
fore August
first.

Road taxes may
be worked out.
Proviso as to
certain road and
other special
taxes.

Certain limita-
tions of this act
not to apply to
road taxes.

keeping an alphabetical list of persons charged with taxes, shall not apply to road taxes.

Ibid § 5.

Powers and liabilities of such collectors.

46. The collector of taxes shall have all the power for the collection of said taxes, during his term of office, heretofore vested in collectors of county taxes under existing laws, and be subject to the same liabilities and penalties for neglect, or violation of the duties of his office.

Ibid § 6

Books to be kept, and names entered in alphabetical order

To be open to inspection, and delivered to successor.

47. The collector of taxes shall provide an appropriate book, the cost of which shall be allowed to him in the settlement of his accounts, in which he shall enter in alphabetical order the names of all persons charged with taxes in the duplicate aforesaid, and showing the amount of such tax charged against each person, which book shall be at all times open to the inspection of each taxpayer, and shall be delivered by the collector of taxes at the expiration of his term to his successor in office.

Ibid § 7

Public notice to be given of the receipt of duplicate.

48. Where any duplicate of taxes assessed is issued and delivered to the collector of taxes, it shall be the duty of said collector to give public notice as soon thereafter as conveniently can be done, by at least ten written or printed notices to be posted in as many public places in different parts of the township or borough, that said duplicate has been issued and delivered to him; and all persons, who shall

Reduction to be made for prompt payment.

within sixty days from the date of said notice make payment of any taxes charged against them in said duplicate, shall be entitled to a reduction of five per centum from the

Penalty on delayed payment.

amount thereof; and all persons, who shall fail to make payment of any taxes charged against them in said duplicate for six months after notice given as aforesaid, shall be charged five per cent. additional on the taxes charged against them, which shall be added thereto by said collector of taxes and collected by him.

Ibid § 8

Days and time fixed for payment and receipt of taxes.

49. The collector of taxes shall, in person or by some person duly authorized, be in attendance for the purpose of receiving and receipting for taxes on Thursday, Friday and Saturday of each week, during the last two weeks of said

67

sixty days, between the hours of two o'clock and six o'clock in the afternoon, at his residence, or some other place in the proper township or borough, to be designated by him in the notice aforesaid. **Place.**

50. The collector of taxes shall collect the taxes charged in said duplicate and pay over the same to the respective treasurers or authorities entitled thereto, after deducting his commission for the collection thereof, which is hereby fixed at two per centum on all taxes paid to him on which an abatement of five per centum is allowed, and at five per centum on all taxes afterwards collected : *Provided*, That where the total amount of taxes charged on a duplicate is less than one thousand dollars, the said collector shall receive three per centum on all taxes paid to him on which an abatement of five per centum is allowed. **Ibid § 9 Compensation of collectors.**

51. Exonerations may be made by the authorities and in the same manner as heretofore. **Ibid §10 Exonerations.**

52. The accounts of collectors of taxes shall be settled by township or borough auditors of the proper township or borough, and he shall state a separate account for each different tax collected by him ; but collectors of county and state taxes shall settle with the county commissioners as heretofore. **Ibid §11 Settlement of accounts.**

53. So much of all general acts heretofore passed, as is inconsistent herewith, is hereby repealed, but this act shall not apply to any taxes, the collection of which is regulated by a local law. **Ibid §13 Repeal. Application of act.**

VII. MISCELLANEOUS.

54. Regulation of burial grounds. When dead may be removed therefrom.
55. Transfer of cemeteries to borough authorities.
56. Overseers and supervisors to give bonds.
57. Office to be vacated in case of default.

54. That authority is hereby vested in the court of quarter sessions of the several counties of this commonwealth to make such orders and degrees for the regulation and care of burial grounds situated in and adjacent to incorpor- **13 May 1876 § 2 P. L. 159. Quarter sessions courts may make orders for care of burial grounds.**

ated boroughs, as the public good shall require; and when
any such burial ground shall become so neglected as, in
the opinion of said court, to become a public nuisance, the

When they may direct removal of dead bodies. court may direct the removal of the dead therefrom, by the
proper borough authorities, to some other properly regula-
ted burial ground, and may enforce, by proper process, or-
ers and decrees made under this act.

Ibid § 3 55. That upon petition of the managers and officers of

Transfer of cemeteries to borough authorities any incorporated cemetery company, and a majority of the
taxables of the borough to which it is proposed to transfer
such cemetery, the said court may authorize the transfer of
any cemetery to the borough authorities of any borough in
which such cemetery may be located or adjacent thereto;
and such transfer shall be made without cost to such borough and upon such transfer being made such borough

Powers of boroughs after transfer made. authorities shall hold and exercise the power and privilege
of such incorporated company, and may purchase lands
within or beyond such borough limits, not to exceed thirty
acres, for the extension of such cemetery, if the same be
deemed necessary, and may raise the means by sale of lots
or otherwise, but in no event by taxation, to pay for the
same, perform such other duties as may be deemed necessary in the premeses; they may lay out the grounds so purchased, and change or alter the original plot of such cemetery, and may dispose of such grounds in the same manner
and for the same purposes as such incorporated company
did or could have done; and a deed made by the burgess
of such borough shall be of the same validity as the deed
of such incorporated company; and the said burgess of any
such borough is hereby authorized to make deeds to those
who heretofore purchased lots for burial, but have not as
yet been furnished with deeds by said cemetery corporations; in changing or altering the plot of such cemetery,
the dead bodies may be removed and re-interred in a suitable place without cost to surviving friends.

16 March 1860 §1 P.L. 174. 56. In this commonwealth it shall be the duty of the
township auditors and borough councils to require the

overseers of the poor and supervisors of roads in each township and borough in this commonwealth, except in the county of Schuylkill, before entering upon their duties, to give bond, with security, to be approved by the auditors or borough councils, in a sum not less than double the probable amount of the tax which may come into the hands of the said officers; which bonds shall be taken in the name of the township or borough, conditioned for the faithful performance of their respective duties as supervisors and overseers of the poor, accounting for and paying over to the township treasurer, or to their successors in office, any balance that may remain in their hands at the settlement of their accounts by the aforesaid auditors or borough councils ; and in case the said officers shall neglect or refuse to pay over said balance remaining in their hands, within thirty days after the settlement, it shall be the duty of the said auditors and borough councils holding the bonds, to proceed, by due course of law, to collect the same for the use of said township or borough: *Provided*, That each officer may give security, individualy, in double the amount of such sum as may, in the judgment of the auditors or borough councils, come unto his hands for the ensuing year; and in such case he shall not be accountable for the acts of his associate in office.

Supervisors and overseers of the poor to give security.

How to be approved.

Bond, relative to.

Each officer may give a separate bond.

57. That any officer or officers failing to give the security required by the first section of this act, within one month after his election, then his or their offices shall be declared vacant, and the court of quarter sessions shall appoint one or more, as the case may be, subject to all the restrictions of the first section of this act, and who shall hold his or their office till the next election ; and until such appointment is made, the officer or officers giving bail shall act for one or more, and if all fail to give the required security, then the preceeding officers shall perform the duties as heretofore, until such appointment is made by the court in accordance with the provisions of this act.

Ibid § 2

Offices declared vacant upon refusal to give bond.

Vacancies, how filled.

DIVISION OF THE BOROUGH INTO FIVE WARDS.

History. March 30, 1885, petition presented to the Court of Quarter Sessions, for the appointment of commissioners to inquire into the propriety of dividing the Borough into five wards. May 11th, 1885, report of commissioners read and confirmed *nisi.*

Wards fixed at five. The commissioners recommended that "The number of the wards be increased to five, that parts of the present wards be erected into one ward and that the residue thereof be divided into four wards, as follows:

First Ward. I.—All that portion of the present West Ward of the Borough of Sunbury, bounded on the north by the southern line of out lots Nos. two (2), three (3),and six (6),on the east by the centre line of Third street, on the south by the centre lrne of Gooseberry alley, and on the west by the Susquehanna river, comprise and be designated the as First Ward.

Second Ward. II.—That all that portion of the present East Ward of the Borough of Sunbury, bounded on the north by the southern line of out-lots Nos. seven (7), and ten (10), on the east by the "Gut," (now known as Spring Run), on the south by the centre line of Chestnut street, and on the west by the centre line of Third street, comprise and be designated as the Second Ward.

Third Ward. III.—That all that portion of the present West Ward, bounded on the north by the centre line of Gooseberry alley, on the east by the centre line of Third street, on the south by the Shamokin creek, and on the west by the Susquehanna river, comprise and be designated as the Third Ward.

Fourth Ward. IV.—That all that portion of the present East Ward, bounded on the north by the centre line of Chestnut street, on the east by the "Gut," (now known as Spring Run), on the south by the Shamokin creek and on the west by the centre line of Third street, comprise and be designated as the Fourth Ward.

71

V.-That all that portion of the present East and West Wards, bounded on the north by the northern line of said borough, being the line of lands of S. P. Wolverton, formerly "Grant's mansion farm," on the east by the "Gut," on the south by the southern line of out-lots ten (10), seven (7), six (6), three (3), and two (2), and on the west by the Susquehanna river, comprise and be designated as the Fifth Ward.

Fifth Ward.

September 9, 1885, exceptions were filed by C. M. Clement, who was also of counsel for the petitioners, the ground and purpose being to defer final confirmation until after the general election.

Confirmation.

December 7, 1835, by leave of Court the exceptions were withdrawn and the following decree made: "This report is confirmed absolutely and it is ordered, adjudged and decreed that each of said Wards be a separate election district, and at the time of the next regular election for borough officers, shall elect two (2) members of the Borough Council, of whom, pursuant to the Act of Assembly, approved June 1, 1883, entitled "An act providing the manner of electing members of town councils in the boroughs of this Commonwealth, and of filling vacancies therein," one half of the whole number of councilmen shall serve for one year, and one-half to serve for two years, and shall annually thereafter elect one-half of the whole number to serve for two years; and shall elect such other public officers as are authorized in boroughs, wards and election districts under existing laws. And that in said Borough there shall be elected annually a Chief Burgess, an Assistant Burgess, three (3) Auditors, two (2) Street Commissioners, one (1) High Constable, and in the manner and at the times provided by law shall elect two (2) Justices of the Peace and two (2) Overseers of the Poor, all of whom shall be elected by the concurrent votes of each ward and whose election shall be ascertained and declared in the manner provided in the Act of Assembly, approved May 10, 1878, entitled "A supplement to an Act to prescribe the manner in which

Officers to be elected annually.

Councilmen.

Other public officers.

Chief burgess assistant burgess, auditors, street commissioners, high constable, justice of the peace, overseers of poor to be elected by concurrent votes of each ward.

courts may divide boroughs into wards, &c." It is further
decreed that each ward shall elect from among the residents of said ward, in the manner prescribed by the Act of
Assembly, approved February 16, 1883, entiled "A further
supplement to an act to prescribe the manner in which the
courts may divide boroughs into wards, &c.," two (2) School
Directors. The places for holding elections shall be as follows: For the First Ward, at the Court House; for the
Second Ward, at the building of C. W. Bassler, on Fourth
street, next his livery office; for the Third Ward, at the
bakery of Landis Fry, situate on Spruce street; for the
Fourth Ward, at the engine house of the Good Intent Fire
Company, on Fourth street; for the Fifth Ward, at the
house of ——————— Cake, known as the Fountain House,
situate on the corner of Packer street and Railroad avenue.
The following named persons are appointed Judges and Inspectors of Election for each ward, to hold the first election
after the division of said borough into wards as aforesaid:
For the First Ward—Judge, Alexander Mantz; Inspectors,
George W. Smith, T. M. Pursel. For the Second Ward—
Judge, W. H. Bright; Inspectors, R. F. Dieffenderfer and
H. D. Bucher. For the Third Ward—Judge, John Lan-
dau; Inspectors, S. S. Hendricks and C. J. Bucher. For
the Fourth Ward—Judge, Jacob Rohrbach; Inspectors, Peter Bowen and Samuel Z. Stroh. For the Fifth
Ward—Judge, F. M. Putman; Inspectors, Wm. T. Renn
and J. J. Anten. H. A. Reed having been elected Assessor
and residing in the First Ward, and S. O. Reed having
been elected Assessor and residing in the Fourth Ward, the
said H. A. Reed will continue to hold the office of Assessor
for the First Ward and S. O. Reed will continue to hold
the office of Assessor for the Fourth Ward, and vacancies
having thereby occurred in the Second, Third and Fifth
Wards, in the office of Assessor, Andrew Hoover is appointed Assessor for the Second Ward, P. M. Shindel is appointed Assessor for the Third Ward, C. T. Bowser is appointed Assessor for the Fifth Ward, and it is further or-

(Marginal notes: School directors. Place for holding elections. Election officers to hold first election. First assessors.)

dered that the assessors of the several wards do proceed forthwith to make a registration of the voters resident in their respective wards, as provided In the general election laws, at least sixty days preceding the next general election. By the Court.

W. M. R., P. J.

BOROUGH ORDINANCES.

————o————

No drains to be cut in river bank.

Resolved, That no person shall be promitted to cut a drain or landing through the bank of the river without the approbation of the regulators and supervisors under the penalty of twenty dollars.

Passed May 18, 1798.

————

AN ORDINANCE.

Regulating the running at large of horses, mares &c.

No horse to be run faster than a canter.

SEC. 1. That no person shall be suffered to run any horse mare or gelding within the borough faster than a cant, under the penalty of fiifteen shillings. If a boy, his father, mother, master or guardian must pay said penalty, unless it shall be proved that said horse carried said boy against his will.

No horse to be ridden faster than a canter.

SEC. 2. That any person or persons that shall or may ride any horse, mare or gelding on any street or alley within the town of Sunbury faster than a canter, shall forfeit and pay the sum of two dollars for every offence.

No bullet match to be played.

SEC. 3. That any person or persons shall or may play at match of bullets, on any street or alley within the town of Sunbury shall forfeit and pay the sum of one dollar for every such offence.

How penalties to be recovered

SEC. 4. That the said fines and penalties shall and may be recovered before any justice of the peace within the said borough, by any person that shall sue for the same, the

one-half thereof to be for the prosecutor and the other half
for the use of the borough. Provided, that the suit be
commenced and brought within twenty-four hours after
such offence shall be committed, and not afterwards.
Passed July 23, 1803.

AN ORDINANCE.

*A Supplement to an Ordinance, passed July 23, 1803, and a
Supplement thereto, passed July 4, 1808, regulating the running at large of horses, mares, geldings, sheep, swine and
geese.*

WHEREAS, The running at large of horses mares, geld- Pream'le.
ings, sheep, swine and geese have been found very detrimental to the convenience of the citizens of the Borough of
Sunbury and contrary to the ordinance, passed July 23,
1803, and the a supplement thereto passed July 4, 1808,
such trespasses are daily committed to the annoyance of
the citizens of the borough aforesaid.

SEC. 1. That it shall be the duty of constable of the borough *Horses, sheep, swine and geese running at large to be impounded by constable and sold after advertisement.*
of Sunbury aforesaid, for the time being, upon seeing and
horses, mares, gelding, sheep, swine or geese running at large
or being not fettered, any of the animals running at large
within any of the streets, alleys or lanes, of the borough
aforesaid, to take up and impound any such animal or animals, and shall give notice by at least six advertisements
posted up in the said borough, at least five days of the taking and impounding, and of the place and time of sale of
such animal or animals, and after having given notice as
aforesaid, he shall sell the animal or animals so taken up
and impounded, unless the designated fines shall be previously paid by the owner or owners of such animal or
amimals, returning the overplus if any, after deducting the
fines and costs to the person or persons who shall prove
themselves to bo the owner or owners of such animal or

Penalty on constable for neglect of duty. animals sold; and upon refusal and neglect of any or all the duties enjoined on the constable aforesaid he shall pay the sum of five dollars, to be recovered before any justice of the peace of the said borough, upon proof made by any one of the inhabitants of the said borough, or other creditable evidence that the running at large of any of the aforesaid animal or animals was within the knowledge or view of the said constable; one-half of such fine shall go to the use of the prosecutor and the residue to the use of the borough aforesaid ; and the said constable shall be entitled to receive the same fees as is allowed constables for making levy and selling property by outcry of execution. &c.

Passed May 26, 1812.

—

AN ORDINANCE.

Relative to colts running at large.

Colts not to run at large. SEC. 1 . That from and after the 14th day of July, instant, it shall be unlawful for colts of any age to run at large witin the limits of the borough of Sunbury, and if any person shall suffer his or her colt to run as aforesaid he or she Penalty. shall pay a fine of ten dollars to the said borough.

SEC. 2. That it shall be the duty of the High Constable upon seeing this ordinance broken, or having notice, to To be impounded and sold. take up and impound any colt so found running at large, and if the owner refuse to pay the said penalty for one day after notice is given the said constable shall sell the same at public vendue after five days notice, and after paying said penalty, all costs and charges, return the overplus if any to the owner.

Fees of constable. SEC. 3. That the constable shall be allowed the same fees for the above services as are allowed for similar proceedings against horses.

Passed May 19, 1838.

AN ORDINANCE.

Whereas, Complainants have been made that a number of boys have been in the habit of assembling in the streets at night and disturbing the peace of the community by shouting and behaving in a disorderly manner therefore.

Preamble. a.

Sec. 1. Be it enacted by the Chief Burgess, Assistant Burgesses and Common Council of the Borough of Sunbury, That if three or more boys, (men or women,) shall be found together in the streets or alleys of the borough after nine o'clock in the evening or at any time, (during the day or night,) shouting and making a noise or trespassing upon other people's property or otherwise behaving in a rude and riotous or disorderly manner, disturbing the peace of the citizens, it shall be the duty of the High Constable to arrest such offenders and convey them before a justice of the peace to be dealt with according to law, and every such person or persons offending shall upon conviction of every such offence forfeit and pay the sum of one dollar, to be recovered with costs of suit before any justice of the peace of said borough, one-half to be paid to the person who shall give the information, and the other to the Chief Burgess for the use of the borough. and for nonpayment of said fines and costs and want of sufficient distress whereof to levy the same it shall be the duty of the High Constable (or constable) having obtained a warrant from a justice of the peace for that purpose, to commit the offender to the common prison, there to remain for the space of 48 hours at hard labor if said fine and costs be not sooner paid.

Three or more boys men and women on streets making a noise or trespassing on people's property, to be arrested and fined.

In default of payment to be committed to jail.

Passed July 17, 1844.

AN ORDINANCE.

Providing for the appointment of a sexton.

Sec. 1. That the Chief Burgess and Assistant Burgesses

---

a. The words in brackets are the amendments adopted May 3, 1881.

78

Sexton to be appointed. Duties.

shall select some person as sexton for the borough of Sunbury and vicinity, whose duty it shall be to take charge of the keys and bier belonging to the grave yard, dress and keep in good order, (i. e.) prevent briers, bushes, grass, &c., from accumulating, for all of which he is to re-

To be compensated.

ceive a reasonable compensation, to be fixed by the aforesaid borough officers.

Passed May 28, 1849.

AN ORDINANCE.

Prohibiting driving, etc., on Market Square.

Riding and driving in Market square prohibited.

SEC. 1. *Be it ordained by the Burgesses, &c.*, That no persons shall under any pretense whatever ride or drive on horseback or in any wagon or wagons, cart or carts, carriage or carriages, or any other vehicle over or across that part of Market Square in the borough east of the Court House, which is surrounded by trees, or cut up the soil

Penalty for violation.

thereon in any manner, under the penalty of one dollar for each offence, to recovered as debts of the same amount are by law recoverable.

Passed May 10, 1852.

AN ORDINANCE.

Prohibiting the running at large of mules or goats.

Mules and goat not to run at large.

SEC. 1. *Be it ordained by the Burgeses, &c.*, That from and after the fifth day of March next. it shall be unlawful for any mule or mules, goat or goats, to run at large in any of the streets, lanes or alleys of the borough of Sunbury, and if any person or persons shall suffer his, her or their mule or mule, goat or goats to run as aforesaid he, she or they shall pay a fine of five dollars for each and every offence for the use of the said borough, and, *Be it further enacted,* That it shall be the duty of the High Constable of the borough aforesaid, to take up and impound any mule or mules, goat or goats, so found running at large, and if the owner or owners refuse to pay the said penalty, after having been duly notified thereof, the said constable shall proceed to sell the same at public vendue, after five days notice by five written or printed handbills of the time and place of sale, and after paying the said penalty, all costs and charges, return the surplus, if any, to the owner or owners thereof, and, *Be it further enacted,* That the aforesaid constable shall be allowed the same fees for the above service as are allowed by the laws of the Commonwealth, to the sheriff for a levy and sale upon execution of property of like amount.

Penalty.

High constable to impound and sell the same.

Overplus to be returned.

Fees.

Passed February 20, 1855.

RESOLUTION.

Granting Northern Central Railway Company right of way.

Resolved, By the Burgesses and Council of the Borough of Sunbury: That the Northern Central Railroad Company be permitted to locate the said road in or through any street, lane or alley in said borough, the said company may deem expedient so to do.

Right of way granted to Northern Central Railway Company.

Passed by council August 27, 1857.

S. J. YOUNG,
Chief Burgess.

Approved by the citizens of the borough at a town meeting held at the Court House.

RESOLUTION.

Granting S. & E. R. R. Co. right of way, without a meeting of Council in Council Chamber.

Right of way granted to Sunbury & Erie Railroad Co., on Deer street.

Resolved by the Burgess and Common Council of the Borough of Sunbury, and it is hereby ordained by the authority of the same; That the Sunbury & Erie Railroad Company shall be permitted to locate and build the said road in or through that portion of Deer street running from Market street to the northern limits of said borough, and the same privileges which were given to the N. C. R. R. Co. by authority of the Burgesses and Council aforesaid, upon the 27th day of August A. D. 1857, be and are hereby extended to the Sunbury & Erie R. R. Co. as aforesaid, so far as the authority of the said Burgess and Council may extend

Borough not to be involved in difficulties.

without involving said borough in difficulties, which may occur from damages or otherwise to the inhabitants thereof. Passed May 3d, 1853.

S. J. YOUNG,
Chief Burgess.

ORDINANCE.

Regulating speed of Locomotives and Trains.

Railroad Companies not to run engines faster than five miles an hour.

Be it ordained by the Burgesses and Common Council of the Borough of Sunbury, and it is hereby enacted by the authority of the same: That on and after this date it shall not be lawful for any railroad company to allow their locomotives or trains of cars to run within the limits of the borough, at a greater speed than at the rate of five miles an hour

Penalty.

under the penalty of twenty-five dollars, for each offence, to

One half to go to prosecutor.

be recovered as debts of same amount. are by law recoverable : one half of said penalty to be paid to the prosecutor,

81

and the other half to be paid to the Borough Treasurer for the use of the borough. Any ordinance relating to the runing of locomotives or trains of cars through the borough, heretofore enacted, is hereby repealed.

Repeal.

Passed June 18, 1859.

J. H. ZIMMERMAN,
Chief Burgess.

AN ORDINANCE

To prevent the selling or exploding of rockets, fire crackers or any other pyrotechnical works in the Borough of Sunbury, Penna.

SECTION 1.—Be it enacted and ordained by the Burgess Assistant Burgesses and Common Councilmen, of the Borough of Sunbury, Pennsylvania, in town council assembled, and it is hereby enacted and ordained by the authority of the same: That if any person or persons within the limits of said borough, shall sell or dispose of any rockets, fire-crackers or any other pyrotechnical works within the limits of said borough, upon conviction thereof before one of the Justices of the Peace in and forsaid borough, shall forfeit and pay a fine of not less than one nor more than fifteen dollars for each and every offence, with costs of suit, the said fines to be recovered with costs of suit before the said Justice, the one-half thereof to be paid to the Borough Treasurer for the use of the said borough, and the other half to the informer or informers.

Sale of fire works prohibited.

Penalty.

SEC. 2.—That if any person or persons shall discharge, set off or explode any rockets, fire crackers or any other pyrotechnical works within the limits of the said borough of Sunbury, upon conviction thereof before one of the Justices of the Peace, in and for said borough, shall each forfeit and pay a fine of one dollar with costs of suit for each and every offence, to be recovered as hereinafter provided.

Discharging of fire works prohibited.

Penalty.

SEC. 3.—That if any person or persons convicted and fined as aforesaid, shall neglect or refuse to make payment of the said fine, together with the costs of suit, it shall be the duty of the said Justice, before whom the said person or persons was or were convicted and fined, to issue a process directed to the High Constable of said borough commanding him to levy the said fines or fine with the costs of suit out of the goods and chattels of the said delinquent, and after ten days' public notice ot such sale by at least six written or printed advertisements, to sell the same to satisfy the said fines and costs. And in the event of the proceeds of said sale exceeding the amount of said fine and costs to pay the overplus to the said defendant. And in case goods and chattels sufficient to satisfy the said fine cannot be found, the High Constable shall, upon a warrant being issued for that purpose by the said justice, take the body or bodies of the said defendant or defendants and convey him or them to the county jail of Northumberland county there to remain for a period of not less than three nor more than ten days, at the option of the said justice, the expense thereof to be borne by the said borough. *Provided, however*, that if the said prisoner or prisoners at any time during his or their incarceration shall pay the amount of said fine or fines and costs as aforesaid he or they shall be immediately discharged and released from the said prison.

(marginal notes: In default of payment, to be levied personal property. When no property can be found defendant to be committed to jail.)

Passed October 2nd, 1860.

GEO. B. YOUNGMAN,
Chief Burgess.

AN ORDINANCE

Prohibiting Drunkness and Disorderly Conduct within the Limits of the Borough of Sunbury.

Be it enacted by the Burgess and Common Councilmen,

of the Borough of Sunbury, and it is hereby enacted by authority of the same: That if any person or persons, within the limits of the borough aforesaid, become intoxicated and disorderly, disturbing the peace, by riotous or other conduct, the Chief Burgess of the said borough, be and is hereby authorized, at his own view, or on information being made before him, to issue a warrant, to cause the arrest of such person or persons so offending against this ordinance, and have the same brought before him, and every such person or persons upon conviction of any such offence, shall forfeit and pay such fine as may be imposed by the Chief Burgess of said borough, not exceeding twenty dollars, for the use of said borough, and any person or persons neglecting or refusing to pay the same with cost of suit, the Chief Burgess is hereby authorized to commit such person or persons to the county jail, for each offence, for any period not exceeding sixty days.

Intoxicated and disorderly persons to be arrested on warrant of Chief Burgess.

Fined by him.

In default to be committed to jail.

Approved December 11th, A. D. 1865.

S. B. BOYER,
Chief Burgess.

AN ORDINANCE

Changing the Names of the Streets in the Borough of Sunbury, Pa.

Whereas, It is deemed expedient to change the names of the several streets in said borough ; therefore,

Be it ordained by the Burgess, Assistant Burgesses and Common Council of the Borough of Sunbury, in town council assembled, and it is hereby enacted by the authority of the same, that the names of the several streets in said Borough of Sunbury shall be altered and changed in the manner following, to-wit: That the street fronting on the

Names of streets changed

river, now called Broadway, shall hereafter be called Front street; the street now called River street shall hereafter be called Second street; the street now called Deer street shall hereafter be called Third street; the street now called Fawn street shall hereafter be called Fourth street; the street now called Short street shall hereafter be called Fifth street; the street now called Elderberry street shall hereafter be called Spruce street; the street now called Whortleberry street shall hereafter be called Walnut street; the street now called Pokeberry street shall hereafter be called Penn street; the street now called Blackberry street shall hereafter be called Chestnut street; the street now called Market or Shamokin street shall hereafter be called Market street; the street now called Dewberry street shall hereafter be called Arch street; the street now called Cranberry street shall hereafter be called Race street; the street recently opened on the south bank of the canal shall be called Vine street; and the street running east and west in Hendricks' Addition shall be called Pine street.

New streets named.

Passed June 5th, 1866.

E. Y. BRIGHT,
Chief Burgess.

AN ORDINANCE

Authorizing a Borough Loan.

Preamble.

Whereas, By the 9th section of the Act of General Assembly of this commonwealth, approved the second day of April, A. D. 1867, entitled, "A further supplement to an Act to erect the Borough of Sunbury, in County of Northumberland, into a borough: it is enacted, "that for the purpose of funding the debt of the borough, and for other borough purposes, as the town council may direct, the said town council are hereby authorized and empowered to borrow any sum or sums of money not exceeding in the aggregate the sum of fifty thousand dollars, and may issue bonds therefor in the corporate name of the borough, payable at such times as the town council may direct, not more than ten years after date, with a rate of interest not exceeding seven per cent., payable semi-annually, and which bonds shall not be taxable for borough purposes. The said bonds shall be signed by the Chief Burgess and attested by the Town Clerk."

Therefore, by the authority of the said Act of Assembly, and in pursuance thereof, be it *Resolved* by the Burgess, Assistant Burgesses and Common Council of the Borough of Sunbury, in the County of Northumberland, in town council assembled, that for the purpose of funding the debt of the borough and for other borough purposes as the town council may direct, the sum of fifty thousand dollars ($50,-000) be borrowed and that bonds be issued therefor in the corporate name of the borough, payable five and ten years after date, with seven per cent. interest, payable semi-annually; and which bonds shall be signed by the Chief Burgess and attested by the Town Clerk, and shall be in the following form, to-wit:

$50,000.00 to be borrowed.

Bonds to be issued.

No.....

BOND OF THE BOROUGH OF SUNBURY, IN THE COUNTY OF NORTHUMBERLAND.

It is hereby certified that the Burgesses and inhabitants of the Borough of Sunbury, in the County of Northumberland are indebted to...... .. .. or bearer, in the sum of one thousand dollars, payable with interest from the first day of July, 1867, inclusive, at seven per cent. per annum, payable on the first day of January and July in each year, on the presentation of the proper coupon hereunto annexed. This debt is authorized by Act of Assembly of the Commonwealth of Pennsylvania, approved the second day of April, A. D. one thousand eight hundred and sixty-

Form of bond

seven, and by a resolution of the town council passed the 7th day of May, 1867.

Sunbury, July 1st, 1867.

. . . .

Chief Burgess.

Attest:

. . . .

Town Clerk.

FORM OF COUPON.

Form of coupon.

The Burgesses and inhabitants of the Borough of Sunbury, in the County of Northumberland, on the first day of . . . ., 18. . . ., will pay to the bearer thirty-four dollars for six months interest on Bond No. . . . . . for one thousand dollars ($1,000.00).

. . . .

Chief Burgess.

Chief Burgess to have bonds printed.

That the Chief Burgess is hereby authorized and empowered to have blank bonds with coupons attached, printed or engraved of the denomination of fifty, one hundred, two hundred, three hundred, five hundred and one thousand dollars each.

May fund debt as direc'ed by council.

And be it further resolved, That the Chief Burgess may from time to. time fund the borough debt, and may give in exchange for all borough bonds hereafter issued, borough orders and bills passed by council, the bonds of the borough hereby authorized to be issued and for such borough purposes as the town council may from time to time direct,,

And seal the bonds.

and the Chief Burgess is hereby authorized to sell the said borough bonds to any person or persons at par to any amount not exceeding the amount hereby authorized to be issued.

Passed May 7th, 1867.

E. Y. BRIGHT,
Chief Burgess.

AN ORDINANCE

Regulating the Markets in the Borough of Sunbury.

SECTION 1.—Be it ordained by the Burgesses and Town Council of the Borough of Sunbury, and it is hereby ordained by authority of the same, that from and after the passage of this ordinance there shall be held two markets in each week during the year, to-wit: On Wednesday and Saturday. The market hours shall be between the hours of four and nine A. M. during the months of May, June, July, August and September, and between the hours of five and ten A. M. during the remainder of the year, and each and every person who shall buy or sell anything in the market before the hours appointed for opening the market aforesaid, shall pay a fine of one dollar for each and every offense and costs. *Provided, however,* that occupants of shops or storehouses or stands on sidewalks within the borough may sell at all hours during secular days, except on market days they shall not sell before regular market hours. *(Markets established. Two days a week. Hours. Penalty for selling before hours.)*

SEC. 2.—No person or persons, shall be permitted to peddle or vend on the streets of this Borough, any eggs, meat, butter, poultry, fruits or vegetables, from wagons, carts or other conveyances, on any day of the week except on regular market days, and on such days only after the hours fixed above for closing the said markets, under a penalty of five dollars for each and every offense. *(Peddling on days other than market days and during market hours prohibited.)*

SEC. 3.—That Market street, from Second to Fifth street, be designated as the market place, extending along the line of the curb from Second street along the south side of Market to Fifth street, thence along the north side of Market street to Second street, be designated as the only limits within which market wagons be allowed to stand within the Borough on said market days. The Clerk of the Market shall set off stations to those desiring to occupy the same regularly, and shall have general supervision over the *(Market street from Second to Fifth on both sides fixed as Market limits. Clerk to assign places have supervision of market.)*

market place, so as not to allow any interference with the stations selected.

Persons not to occupy stations without permission. SEC. 4.—That no one shall be allowed to occupy any station selected on said market days unless by permit from the regular occupant or the Clerk of the Market, and any person or persons violating this section shall be fined one dollar for each and every offense.

Clerk to keep streets clean and level snow. SEC. 5.—It shall be the duty of the Clerk of the Market to keep the street cleansed of all rubbish, refuse or any dirt left on them by the market wagons, and in the winter to have the snow leveled so that wagons and other vehicles can conveniently back up to the curb, and see that meat butter and other marketing sold by the pound is weighed **Spring balance prohibited.** upon scales; the use of spring balances in said market being hereby prohibited, and it shall be his duty to prosecute for **Clerk to try all provisions purporting to be of good weight and condemn deficient.** all breaches thereof. He shall weigh, try and examine all bread, butter, lard and other provisions purporting to be of a given weight or measure, which are found in the market, and if found deficient in weight shall seize the same and condemn it for the use of the said Borough.

No provisions to be bought during market hours for retailing. SEC. 6.—That no person shall, during market hours, buy or cause to be bought, any articles of provisions, fruit, or other commodity whatever for the purpose of retailing the same.

Articles of less weight than represented to be forfeited. SEC. 7.—That if any person or persons shall sell or bring, to market for sale, any bread, butter, lard, fruit or other provisions, in lumps, loaves, tubs, vessels or parcels, as or for a greater weight or measure than the true weight or measure thereof, or shall supply any device for imposition or fraud in the sale of any provisions, the said articles so offered for sale, shall be forfeited to the use of the Borough.

Tainted meat and other food and veal under four weeks old to be forfeited. SEC. 8.—That all beef, pork, mutton, lamb, veal, and all kinds of. poultry and fish, and all other articles of food whatever, that shall be brought to the market or publicly exposed to sale in the Borough, and shall be found diseased tainted, or in any manner rendered unwholesome or unfit for

89

use, and all veal which when killed shall not have been of the age of four weeks, be forfeited, and the person or persons exposing the same for sale shall moreover, in connection thereof, forfeit and pay a fine of five dollars for the use of the Borough.

Parties to be fined.

SEC. 9.—That for any and every infraction or violation of any of the provisions of this Ordinance (not otherwise provided for,) the offender or offenders shall be fined in any sum not less than three, nor more than ten dollars, at the discretion of the Burgess, or any Justice of the Peace of the said Borough, before whom the offenders may be prosecuted to conviction. All fines imposed by this Ordinance shall be recovered as herein provided for, and shall be paid into the Borough Treasury.

Fines, how imposed.

To be paid into the treasury.

SEC. 10.—That all market Ordinances heretofore passed and unconsistant herewith, are hereby repealed. And be it further ordained by the Burgess and Town Council; That one suitable person, a citizen of the said Borough of Sunbury, shall be appointed by the Burgess and Town Council, as Clerk of the Market, for said Borough, who shall attend all market days, and cause and regulate the market fully as stipulated in the Ordinances regulating the markets. To cause a record to be kept of each day's proceedings, at the end of every three months, and at the expiration of his term of office, his accounts shall be audited by the Auditing Committee of the Borough.

Repeal.

Clerk to be appointed.

Duties.

SEC. 12.—That the said Clerk of the Market shall receive the sum of two dollars and fifty cents for every day in attendance on said market days.

a.

By order of the Council,

D. HEIM,
Chief Burgess.

---

a The compensation of the Clerk is now fixed at one-half of the receipts from the occupiers of stations, and each person standing in Market pays ten cents per week for that privilege, this change was made by resolution.

Be it further ordained by the Burgess and Town Council
Day· fix·d at
thre . of the Borough of Sunbury, That the market days be so
amended as to make three market days, Tuesdays, Thursdays and Saturdays instead of Wednesdays and Saturdays,
and to close at 8 o'clock for the butchers.
May 7th., 1872.

SOL. MALICK,
Chief Burgess.

AN ORDINANCE.

*To provide for the election of Chief Engineer and assistants for
Fire Department and defining their duties.*

Fire department created.

a.

SEC. 1.—Be it ordained by the Burgesses and Councilmen or Sunbury, in town council assembled, That several
Fire Companies of the Borough of Sunbury accepting the
provisions of the ordinance and such others as may be admitted in the manner hereinafter prescribed shall be known
and designated by the title of the Sunbury Fire Department.

Officers.

SEC. 2.—The officers of the Fire Departments shall consist of a Chief Engineer and First and Second assistant
Engineers.

Delegates of
department.

SEC. 3.—Three persons shall be elected by each company
at their stated meetings proceeding the fourth Monday of
June in each and every year, who shall serve as delegates of
Sunbury fire department. The said delegates shall have full

Power of delegat·s.

power and authority to adopt such rules and regulations in
addition to this ordinance for the government of said department, as they may consider necessary ; to admit other companies into the department, to elect the officers of the depart-

To elect officers

ment, to impose such penalties for dereliction of duty and
misconduct as they may see fit, and to remove from office
for incompetancy or gross neglect. Provided, Their actions

---

a. No action has yet been taken by the Companies under this ordinance,
but it can be acted under at any time.

shall be communicated to council and approved by them.
A majority of all the delegates shall constitute a quorum for
the transaction of business. A majority of all the votes of
the delegates present shall be necessary to a decision or
election.

Quorum and majority.

SEC. 4.—The election for Chief Engineer and Assistants
shall be held on the fourth Monday of August in each year,
at the council chamber at 7.30 o'clock P. M. Returns of
said election shall be sent to the several companies and council
without delay.

When election to be held.

SEC. 5.—The Chief Engineer in all cases of fire or alarm
shall have the whole control and commands of all the fire
companies and the apparatuses. The First Assistant Engineer shall, in the absence of the Chief Engineer, be invested
with all the power conferred upon that officer. In the absence
of both, the Second Assistant Engineer shall take command,
and if all the above named officers are absent the commanding officers of each company shall have full authority to act.

Powers of chief engineer and assistants

SEC. 6.—It shall be the duty of the Chief Engineer to
exercise a careful supervision over all the borough property
occupied and in use by the different fire companies and to
report in writing to council any destruction, rash neglect or
abuse of the same forthwith. He shall also on the first
Tuesday of August and February in each year, send in a
written report of number of feet of hose, buckets etc., in
possession of each company fit for service, and the condition
of the building and apparatus.

Duties of chief engineer

To report on condition of apparatus, &c.

SEC. 7.—The Chief and Assistant Engineer before assuming any of the duties of their respective offices shall be duly
sworn before the Chief Burgess and councilmen by him.

To be sworn.

SEC. 8—The Chief and Assistant Engineers shall receive
such compensation for their services as may from time to
time be fixed by council.

Compensation.

Passed July 6th, 1880.

A. X. BRICE,
Chief Burgess.

AN ORDINANCE

To provide for the certain extinguishment of the borough debt and expenditure of the revenue.

SECTION 1.—Be it ordained by the Burgesses and Councilmen of the Borough of Sunbury, in town council assembled :

No money to be expended without appropriation. No money shall be drawn from the treasury of the borough unless the same shall be previously appropriated by council to the purpose for which it is drawn.

Regular appropriations to be made for ordinary expenses. SEC. 2.—The council shall provide for the payment of debts and expenses of the borough by regular appropriations made before the commencement of the fiscal year, during which the moneys appropriated are to be expended, and, shall make extra and special appropriations when they deem the same necessary ; Provided, No ordinance appropriating money shall be passed finally at the same session at which it *Majority of the whole required for passage of appropriation ordinance.* was introduced, nor go into effect, unless on its final passage a majority of the Burgesses and councilmen elected shall vote in its favor, which vote shall be by yeas and nays and the names of those voting shall be entered upon the minutes. *Provided,* Further orders may be granted in pursuance of any appropriation regularly made by the vote of the majority present.

Chief Burgess not to suffer appropriations to be overdrawn nor sign orders in excess thereof. SEC. 3.—The Chief Burgess shall not suffer any appropriation made by the council to be over drawn. Every case when an appropriation shall be exausted and the object of which is not completed, he shall immediately report to the council with a statement of the money which may have been drawn on such appropriation and the purpose for which they were drawn. He shall not sign any orders in excess of the amount of any appropriations.

Accounts to be opened for each appropriation. SEC. 4.—The Town Clerk shall open and keep under appropriate titles as many accounts as may be necessary to show distinctly and separately all moneys expended under every appropriation made by council.

All bills to be SEC. 5.—No order shall be granted for supplies furnished or services performed except upon a voucher duly written in ink, setting forth the particular date and items of charge, and approved by the proper officer or committee. *in ink and approved before order granted.*

SEC. 6.—The Overseers of the Poor shall ascertain and determine the probable amount that will be required for the support of the poor during the ensuing year and certify the same to the council on or before the 31st day of March in each year, and the council shall revise the same and appropriate such sum as may be necessary for the support and maintainance of the poor as herein before provided. The Overseers shall expend the moneys so appropriated, as judiciously as may be, by orders drawn on the Borough Treasurer signed by two of the Overseers, and shall report monthly to the council a statement of the orders drawn by them during the preceeding month. *Overseers to estimate probable cost of supporting the poor and report to council.* *To submit monthly statement of orders granted.*

SEC. 7.—Should any appropriation be exausted, and it shall appear to the council to be necessary and for the best interest of the borough, they shall make an extra appropriation for that purpose. Unexpended balances of appropriations shall be covered into the treasury at the end of the year. *When appropriation exausted, extra appropriation may be made.*

SEC. 8.—The fiscal year shall end on the second Monday of March of each and every year, on or before which day every officer or agent of the borough charged with the reception or collection of borough moneys shall settle his accounts with the Borough Treasurer, pay to him all moneys of the borough in his hands or custody. *End fiscal year and all officers to settle with treasurer.*

SEC. 9.—This ordinance shall go into effect immediately Provided ; services rendered and supplies furnished before this date or before the passage of the ordinance making the appropriations for the current year shall be paid for as heretofore provided, the vouchers be therefore presented within thirty days from the passage of this ordinance. *Proviso for current year.*

Passed May 3d, 1881.

W. C. PACKER,
Chief Burgess.

94

AN ORDINANCE

To provide for the redemption and refunding of the borough debt, by issuing new bonds therefor.

SECTION 1.—Be it ordained by the Burgesses and inhabitants of the Borough of Sunbury in Town Council assembled,

Indebtedness to be refunded. That the bonds and interests bearing evidences of indebtedness of the borough be redeemed and paid, and for the purpose of redeeming and paying such bonds and indebtedness

a. that bonds be issued, with interest coupons attached, payable semi-annually, bearing interest at the rate of four and

Bonds to be issued at 4½ per cent payable in twenty years, redeemable at option after five years. one-half [4½] per cent. per annum, redeemable at the option of the Borough after five years, and payable at any time within twenty years from and after the date thereof, amounting to the sum of forty-five thousand dollars, [$45,000,] (or so much thereof as may be necessary for the purpose of re-

a. The regulations passed for carrying this ordinance into effect, and not fully executed in the paying of the loan, as follows:

SEC. 1. Resolved, That the bonds so issued shall be of the following numbers and amounts, twenty-two of said bonds shall be numbered from number one to number twenty-two inclusive and shall each be for the sum of one thousand dollars, thirty-eight of said bonds shall be numbered from number twenty-three to number sixty inclusive and shall be for the sum of five hundred dollars each, forty of said bonds shall be numbered from number sixty-one to number one hundred inclusive and shall be for the sum of one hundred dollars each

SEC. 2. Said bonds and the coupons attached shall be in the following form:

No............   UNITED STATES OF AMERICA. $............
STATE OF PENNSYLVANIA.   BOROUGH OF SUNBURY.
NORTHUMBERLAND COUNTY.

The Borough of Sunbury is indebted to the bearer to the sum of dollars, payable at the office of the Borough Treasurer on the first day of November, A. D. 1901, with interest at the rate of four and one-half per centum per annum, payable on the first day of May and November in each year, on presentation at the office of the Borough Treasurer of the proper coupon hereunto attached. The said Borough reserving the option of paying and redeeming this bond at any time after five years from the date hereof. The said borough guarantees that the sum of two thousand dollars shall be set apart annually out of the moneys collected by taxation in said year as a fund to be applied to the payment and redemption of the loan of which this bond secures a part, and further guarantees the payment of all taxes for State purposes as-

deeming and paying such outstanding,bonds and indebted.
ness,) and that said bonds so issued shall be exempt from
all taxation.

SEC. 2.—That the sum of two thousand dollars be set
apart annually, as a sinking fund for the payment of said
bonds, out of the moneys collected by taxation in said year,
which fund shall be invested solely in said bonds, o r the
bonds of the United States, State of Pennsylvania or County
of Northumberland, and that the creation and inviolable
maintainance of said sinking fund be made a part of the
contract, and embodied in said bonds.

SEC. 3.—That the Borough of Sunbury guarantee the payment of all taxes for State purposes which may be assessed
upon said bonds.

SEC. 4.—That the said bonds be executed by the Chief
Burgess, and attested by the Town Cl erk under the corpor-

---

sessed upon said loan and this bond. This bond is one of one hundred amounting in the aggregate to forty-five thousand dollars, issued and executed in pursuance of the acts of Assembly in such case provided and the ordinance and
resolution of the Council of the borough of Sunbury.

In testimony whereof the said Borough of Sunbury has caused its corporate
seal to be hereunto affixed, and the name to be signed by
| CORPORATE
its Chief Burgess and attested by its Clerk at Sunbury, and
bearing date the first day of November, Anno Domini,
SEAL.
one thousand eight hundred and eighty-one.

....Chief Burgess.
....Town Clerk.
Exempt from taxation except for State purposes by law.
Bond.   No.
The Borough of Sunbury will pay to the bearer on the first day of
A. D., 18 , on presentation·of this coupon the sum of   dol-
lars, six months interest due on Bond numbered as above for
dollars.   ....Clerk.

SEC. 3. Forty coupons of the form above set out shall be attached to each
l ond, each for the amount of the semi-annual interest thereon payable sever-
ally on the first day of May and November in each year, said coupons to be
numbered consecutively from one to forty inlcusive in addition to the number
of the bonds. * * * * *

SEC. 14. There shall be provided a well bound blank book, containing at
least one leaf for each of said bonds. The Treasurer shall enter upon the
leaf so appropriated to such bond, the number and amount thereof, the name

ate seal of the borough and placed in the hands of the Borough Treasurer for delivery in accordance with, and subject to such regulations and resolutions as the council may adopt for the sale and delivery thereof and the payment and redemption of the said outstanding indebtedness.

W. C. PACKER.
Chief Burgess.

AN ORDINANCE

To grant the right of way on Penn street for a double track railroad to the Shamokin, Sunbury & Lewisburg R. R. Co.

SECTION 1.—Be it ordained by the Burgesses and inhabitants of the Borough of Sunbury, in town council assembled: That the right of way to erect, construct and maintain a double track railroad with the necessary switches, transfer and connecting tracks, through and over Penn street in said borough, be and the same is hereby granted to the Shamokin, Sunbury & Lewisburg R. R. Co., its successors and assigns free and discharged from all claims on account of damages that may be sustained by the Borough of Sunbury.

SEC. 2.—The Chief Burgess is hereby authorized and empowered to make, execute and deliver to the said Shamokin,

Right of way granted on Penn St, to the S. S. & L. R.R. Co.

of the person to whom issued, the date of issue and whether for cash or in exchange for outstanding indebtedness.

SEC. 15. Thereafter it shall be the duty of the Borough Auditors, annually, to plainly and effectually cancel all coupons for interest, upon said bonds paid by the Treasurer and thereupon to securely attach the same, consecutively, with mucilage or other paste, to the leaf set apart to the respective bonds; and upon the payment of the principal upon any bond, the same shall be in like manner cancelled and attached to said leaf.

SEC. 16. The Chief Burgess and Borough Auditors shall constitute a committee, whose duty shall be to see to the investment of the sinking fund, and that the proceeds of said fund and all interest thereon, be from time to time applied to the payment and redemption of said bonds. A detailed statement of said fund, how the same is invested, and the application thereof, shall be published annually with the Auditor's Report.

Sunbury & Lewisburg R. R. Co. under the corporate seal of
said borough,attested by the Town Clerk and acknowledged
in due form of law, a good sufficient grant, release and assurance of the rights and privileges hereby granted or intended so to be.

Passed April 5th, 1882.

W. C. PACKER,
Chief Burgess.

AN ORDINANCE

*To grant the privilege of erecting wharves on the river bank to
the S. S. & L. R. R. Co.*

SECTION 1.—Be it ordained by the Burgesses and inhabitants of the Borough of Sunbury, in town council assembled:
That in consideration of the benefits to be derived by the
inhabitants from the construction of said railroad, the use
of so much of the river bank as lies west of the eastern line
of the protecting bank and south of Penn street, as may be
necessary for the purpose of shipping coal by canal, be and
the same is hereby granted to the Shamokin, Sunbury &
Lewisburg R. R. Co. with the privilege of erecting and
maintaining thereon such depots, wharves, piers, schutes,
tracks and switches as may be useful and requisite in and
about their business of shipping coal by canal on Shamokin
Dam. *Provided,* that the company shall from time to time
and at all times hereafter keep the said protecting bank
lying along, back of or under their wharves in perpetual
good order and repair.

SEC. 2.—The Chief Burgess is hereby authorized and empowered to make, execute and deliver to the said Shamokin,
Sunbury & Lewisburg Railroad Company under the corporate seal of said borough, attested by the Town Clerk and
acknowledged in due form of law, a good sufficient grant

Privilege to erect wharves on river bank & L. R. R. Co.

and release and assurance of the rights and privileges hereby granted or intntended to be.

Passed April 15th, 1882.

W. C. PACKER,
Chief Burgess.

AN ORDINANCE

Prohibiting Blocking Streets, Sidewalks &c., and Empowering Policemen to make Arrests for same.

Be it ordained by the Burgesses and inhabitants of Sunbury in town council assembled, that if any person shall by standing or congregating upon the streets, alleys, pavements and sidewalks of the borough, obstruct or blockade the same, or interfere with the citizens of the State passing or repassing, riding or walking along the same, or if any men or boys shall habitually, idly gather together at any one place and there loiter about to the common nuisance of the inhabitants of the borough it shall be the duty of the policemen, constables and other borough officers to notify such persons so offending to move on, clear the streets or abate the nuisance forthwith, and upon failure so to do they shall be arrested by the said policeman or other officers, and upon conviction before any justice of the peace shall pay a fine not to exceed five dollars, and in default thereof to undergo an imprisonment for forty-eight hours in the common jail.

Persons obstructing street or idly loitering about to be required to clear the street or arrested and fined.

In default to be imprisoned.

Passed November 28th, 1882.

W. C. PACKER,
Chief Burgess.

AN ORDINANCE

Requiring Overseers of the Poor to give Bonds before Entering upon their Duties.

Whereas, it is provided by an Act of Assembly entitled

"An Act requiring Supervisors of Roads and Overseers of Preamble.
the Poor in this Commonwealth to give security," approved
16th March, 1860, that it is the duty of borough councils
to require Overseers of the Poor before entering upon their
duties to give bonds with security to be approved by the
Council in a sum not less than double the probable amount
of the tax which may come into the hands of the said officers; and whereas, the Overseers of the Poor of the Borough of Sunbury, although not receiving any taxes into
their hands, do expend by the orders upon the Borough
Treasurer the money set apart for poor purposes with like
effect as if they had collected the sum; therefore,

SECTION 1.—Be it ordained by the Burgesses and inhabitants of the Borough of Sunbury in Town Council assem-
bled, that annually hereafter the Overseers of the Poor of [Overseers to give bonds in $5,000.]
the Borough of Sunbury be required before entering upon
their duties to give bonds in the sum of five thousand dollars conditioned for the faithful performance of their duties as Overseers of the Poor and the accounting for all
sums by them expended by orders on the Borough Treasurer.

SEC. 2.—That no orders of the said Overseers, and no or- [No orders to be drawn, or paid before security given.]
der for the payment of money drawn and signed by the
Overseers of the Poor, shall be binding on the borough until such bond and security are given, and the Borough
Treasurer shall not pay any order granted after April 1st,
1883, until the said bond and security shall be given.

SEC. 3.—This ordinance shall take effect immediately and
the Overseers elected for the ensuing year shall be notified
by the Chief Burgess to give bond within ten days hereafter. *Provided*, that hereafter annually the said bond and
security shall be given within the time provided by the
Act of Assembly.

Passed March 29th, 1883.

W. C. PACKER,
Chief Burgess.

100

AN ORDINANCE

For Making a Public Park.

River bank from Race to Chestnut declared a public park.

SECTION 1.—Be it ordained by the Burgesses and Town Council of the Borough of Sunbury, in Town Council assembled, that so much of the river bank as is shown and represented by the plan drawn by R. H. Faries, extending from near Race street on the north to near Chestnut on the south, and from Front or First street to low water mark of river, be and the same is hereby declared a public park to be used and enjoyed as such forever.

To be graded and fenced, reserving roadway of 50 feet.

SEC. 2.—That the citizens of the said borough contributing to that purpose be and are hereby authorized to enter upon, fence, lay out inside and fill up said park in such manner as they may deem proper, reserving always a roadway of fifty feet in width from along the line of the houses on said Front street.

Whole bank to S. S. & L. R. R. included.

SEC. 3.—That the whole of the river bank from the tracks of the S., S. & L. R. R. to Race street be included in the said park on the expiration of the present leases.

Passed July 5th, 1883.

W. C. PACKER,
Chief Burgess.

———

AN ORDINANCE

Granting the Right of Way for a Sewer through Barberry Alley.

Right of way for sewer in Barberry alley.

Be it ordained by the Burgess and inhabitants of the Borough of Sunbury in Town Council assembled, that a right of way be granted for the construction of a common sewer running from Third street through Main (Barberry) alley to the Susquehanna river, under the direction of the

Borough Engineer and the Committee on Streets and Alleys, the borough to have the right to connect with said sewer.

Passed September 5th, 1883.

W. C. PACKER,
Chief Burgess.

AN ORDINANCE

For the Extension of Second Street and to Regulate the Pavements and Roadways thereof.

SECTION 1.—Be it ordained by the Burgess and inhabitants of the Borough of Sunbury in Town Council assembled, that the public road lately laid out by order by the Court of Quarter Sessions of the Peace of Northumberland county, from the northern line of Race street to intersect a public road known as Railroad avenue, be and the same is hereby taken and accepted as a public street by the said borough, the same to be hereafter known and designated by the name and style of Second street. *(Second street extended from Race to Railroad Avenue.)*

SEC. 2.—The width of the roadway of Second street from the northern line of Race street to the south line of Railroad avenue shall be forty feet and the pavements and sidewalks shall be five feet, and no bulk, bay or jut windows, porches, cellar doors or steps shall be made or set up and constructed in or upon the said pavements or sidewalks or within twenty-five feet of the center line of said street. *(Width of roadway and sidewalks fixed. Bay windows, porches and cellar doors on streets prohibited.)* *Provided*, that porches, steps and cellar doors now extending upon said street shall not be hereby declared a nuisance, but in the event of the reconstruction, altering or repairing of any building now erected the same shall be made to conform in all respects to the provisions of this ordinance.

SEC. 3.—It is hereby declared to be the purpose of this ordinance to make uniform roadways and sidewalks *(Intent.)*

throughout the whole and entire length of Second street.
. Passed December 4th, 1883.

W. C. PACKER,
Chief Burgess.

AN ORDINANCE.

Granting the Right of Way through certain Streets of the Borough of Sunbury to The Sunbury and Northumberland Street Railway Company.

Be it enacted and ordained by the Burgesses and Town Council of the Borough of Sunbury, in Town Council met, and it is hereby enacted and ordained by the authority of the same:

Right of way on several streets from Pine to borough line granted to Sunbury & Northumberland Street Railway Company.

FIRST.—That license and liberty be granted to "The Sunbury and Northumberland Street Railway Company" to locate, erect and construct a street passenger railway in, through and upon the following streets and highways of the said borough, to-wit: Beginning on Second street at its intersection with Pine street, north on Second street to its intersection with Line street; west on Line street to its intersection with Railroad avenue; north on Railroad avenue to its intersection with Packer or Julia street; west on Packer or Julia street to Susquehanna avenue; and north on Susquehanna avenue to the northern line of the borough. Also, beginning on Market street at its intersection with Second street, east to Fourth street, occupying both sides of the said Market street, around the Market Square Park; north on Fourth street from its intersection with Market street to Arch street; and on Arch street from its intersection with Fourth street west to Second street, subject to the terms, condition and restrictions hereinafter provided.

SECOND.—Before entering upon or breaking ground in

any of the said streets, for the purpose of this grant, the Company to file bond in said railway company shall file a bond with sufficient sure- condition for damages. ties, to be approved by the said Borough Council, in the sum of five thousand dollars, conditioned to pay all damages, public or private, that may accrue by reason of the location, erection and construction of the said street passenger railway.

THIRD.—The grades of the said several streets and high- Grades of streets not to ways to be used and occupied by the said company as afore- be changed and track to con- said in the pursuit of any of the erections or structures of form thereto at all times. the said company for the purposes aforesaid, shall in no instance be changed or altered, except under the special direction and supervision of the said Borough Council, by resolution or ordinance for the purpose first duly enacted or adopted; and in any instance or event the said railway and its tracks shall strictly conform to the existing grades of the said streets or highways, unless they be changed or altered by the authority aforesaid; in which event the said railway and its tracks shall be so fixed, laid and adjusted as to conform strictly to the said changed or altered grades. And the said railway company shall, at any and all times hereafter, at its own proper charge and expense, take up, change and alter its railroad so as to conform to such grades, heighths and slopes as the Council may from time to time fix, appoint, renew, alter, change and determine for said streets or highways occupied as aforesaid.

FOURTH.—That in the event the said company shall be Should council authorize a authorized as aforesaid to raise or cut down the grade of change of grade the company to its road differing from the existing grades of the said make such change at its streets, in the pursuit of its erections and structures afore- own cost. said, it shall be incumbent on the said company to adjust the grades of the streets or highways for common travel and public use, on each side of its track or tracks, so as strictly to conform to the grade of the said track or tracks as these shall be located upon the ground, by filling or excavation, at the sole cost and exclusive expense of the said company, such roadway for common use and public travel to be so graded equally with the said railway and track or tracks to a width of not less than twelve feet on each side thereof; and if any street, lane or alley of the said borough, through which the said railway in its route shall pass, shall be and exist of such a width as will not permit of the construction on each side of the track or tracks of the said railway, of a roadway of a width of twelve feet, as aforesaid, then and in that event the said railway company shall, at its own proper cost, charge and expense, cause such street, lane or alley to be opened of the width at least equal to that of such street, lane or alley so occupied by its railway, exclusive of the ground so occupied by it as the same shall then exist.

Twelve feet of roadway to be graded on each side of track except streets of lesswidth there than full width of street be graded to.

FIFTH.—That the said railway company be required to keep in repair its roadbed or roadway in all the streets and highways to be used and occupied by it as aforesaid, and so to construct and maintain its track or tracks between the rails, as well as on both sides thereof for the space of at least two (2) feet outside the rails, that driving on, off, or across the said track or tracks with ordinary vehicles may be safe and not inconvenient, and shall be so laid and constructed as not to impede travel with horses and wagons along or across the said rails.

Tracks to be so laid, as to admit of riding or driving on or across the same without inconvience.

SIXTH.—That the said Railway Company be required to promptly remove the surplus ground, earth, debris, or other materials which may interfere with the proper and equal grading of the streets, or railway, while the latter shall be in course of construction; and if by any means, or advent-ure, the said Company should, at any time after construction or commencement thereof, abandon its enterprise, or improvement, at its own expense the tracks shall be removed promptly, as well as all other materials, or debris, and the said streets left in good repair and condition for public use, and not inferior to the condition thereof when so first used and occupied by the said Company, as aforesaid.

Company to remove all debris and in event of abandonment to remove its tracks.

SEVENTH.—In the event of fire, or the alarm of fire, right

of way must be yielded readily and at once to the Fire-en- Fire apparatus to have right of way. gines and hose carriages, and the Company shall not by the running of its cars, or in any other way, interfere with the proper and necessary use of the said Fire-engines, hose carriages, hose, or hook and ladder trucks.

EIGHTH.—Nor shall the said Company make use of any Streets or alleys not to be used as places of deposit. of the streets, lanes, or alleys of the said Borough as standing room for their cars or horses, or as places of deposit for any property or material whatever. They shall attach Alarm to be attached to horse or car. bells to the horses, or other animals, drawing their cars, or provide some other suitable and adequate alarm that will warn those approaching, crossing, or moving on, or along the track or tracks, or in proximity to the same, of the approach of the car.

NINTH.—It being the true interest of this ordinance to supply and take the place of the ordinance adopted the fifth day of October A. D., 1886, the same is hereby repealed, and its provisions and restrictions are hereby declared null and void. And the Chief Burgess is hereby authorized and empowered to make, execute and deliver a grant of the privileges passed, or intended to be, according to the provisions of this ordinance unto the said Railway Company, and to affix the corporate seal of the said Borough thereto, and the Town Clerk is hereby authorized to sign and attest the same in the usual form of executing such instruments of writing.

Passed February 1, 1887.

GEO. M. RENN,
Chief Burgess.

AN ORDINANCE.

To repeal certain ordinances and parts of ordinances.

SECTION 1. Be it ordained by the Burgesses and inhabitants of the borough of Sunbury, in town council assembled,

Certain ordin-
ances and parts
of ordinances
repealed.

That the ordinance passed May 15, 1824, repealing so much of the ordinance passed July 23, 1804. and the several supplements thereto as respected the running at large of sheep and geese, be and the same is hereby repealed.

SECTION 2. That the following ordinances be and the same are hereby repealed, ordinance passed March 3, 1857, entitled "an ordinance to provide for the paving of the side walks and crossings of Shamokin or Market street in the borough of Sunbury," an ordinance passed June 20,1859, entitled "an ordinance for paving Fawn and Blackberry streets", and an ordinance passed July 5, 1869, entitled, "an ordinance for the paving of Market street", and an ordinance passed June 9, 1800, to regulate the width of porches and steps and of the pavements and sidewalks, also an ordinance passed November 3, 1826, entitled "an ordinance for more effectually preventing Exhibitions and Performances of various kinds in the borough of Sunbury." also the supplement thereto passed Sept. 19,1864, entitled "an ordinance relative to places of amusement ;" also an ordinance passed August 6, 1867, entitled, "an ordinance relative to circuses, &c ;" also an ordinance passed May 19, 1838, "to provide penalties for certain nuisances;" also an ordinance passed May 24, 1859, entitled, "an ordinance relative to nuisances in streets, lanes and alleys," also an ordinance passed June 30, 1859, entitled "an ordinance relative to digging gutters, &c.," also an ordinance passed July 16, 1859, entitled "an ordinance to prohibit the throwing of nuisances into the Basin and Gut ;" also an ordinance passed May 5, 1863, entitled "an ordinance to grade, macadamize, pave, gutter, &c., Broadway, Deer, Fawn Cranberry, Blackberry, Whortleberry, River and Market streets ;" also an ordinance passed June 5, 1866, entitled "an ordinance to direct and regulate the grading, paving curbing and guttering of the side or foot walks of the borough of Sunbury ;" also an ordinance passed August 6, 1867, entitled "an ordinance relative to public places of amusement, closing saloons, &c ;" also an ordinance passed August 6, 1867, entitled "an ordinnance authorizing the appointment of special police;" also an ordinance passen February 3, 1873, entitled " an ordinance to direct and require the occupants of real estate to keep the streets free from coal ashes, &c."; also an ordinance passed June 18, 1872, entitled "an ordinance regulating Market square in the borough of Sunbury"; also an ordinance passed February 4, 1873, entitled "an ordinance to require the keeping of the sidewalks clear of snow, &c."; also an ordinance passed February 3, 1873, entitled "an ordinance for paving west side Chestnut street from Fourth to Second street, and Second street on the west side from Walnut to Pine and the west side of Short street"; also an ordinace passed June 8, 1881, entitled "an ordinance relative to the filling up of sink holes, water ponds and removal of privy vaults and other nuisances"; also an ordinance passed June 5, 1883, entitled "an ordinance for the guttering of Third street."

Passed Feb. 11, 1887.

G. M. RENN,
Chief Burgess.

AN ORDINANCE.

To provide for the prevention and abatement of nuisances and the punishment of the offenders.

SECTION 1.—Be it enacted and ordained, by the Burgesses Inhabitants and of the Borough of Sunbury, in town council assembled, and it is enacted and ordained by the authority of the same. That whatever is dangerous to human life or health, whatever renders the air or food or water or other drinks unwholesome, and whatever buildings, erection, or part or cellar thereof, is overcrowded, or not provided with adequate means of ingress and egress, or is not sufficiently supported, ventilated, sewered, drained, cleaned or lighted are declared to be nuisances, and to be illegal; and every per-

Nuisances defined.

son having aided in creating or contributing to the same, or who may support, continue or retain any of them shall be deemed guilty of a violation of this ordinance and also be liable for expenses of the abatement and remedy therefor, and a penalty not exceeding twenty dollars.

Offenders to abate the same and be subject to penalty.

Sec. 2.—No house-refuse, offal, garbage, dead animals, decaying vegetable matter, or organic waste substance of any kind, shall be thrown upon any street, road, ditch, gutter, public place, vacant lots or the Spring Run or Gut, and no putrid or decaying animal or vegetable matter shall be kept in any house, cellar or adjoining outbuildings for more than twenty-four hours. Violation of any of the provisions of this section shall be punished by a fine of not exceeding than twenty dollars.

House refuse, garbage, etc., not to be exposed, or kept in any building for more than 24 hours.

Sec. 3.—No person or company shall erect or maintain any manufactory or place of business dangerous to life or detrimental to health. or where unwholesome, offensive or deleterious odors, gas, smoke, deposit or exhalations are generated, without the permit of the town council, and all such establishments shall be kept clean and wholesome so as not to be prejudicial to public health, nor shall any deleterious waste-substance, refuse or injurious matter be allowed to accumulate upon the premises or be thrown or allowed to run into any public waters, stream, water course, street, road or public place. And every person or company conducting such manufacture or business shall use the best approved and all reasonable means to prevent the escape of smoke, gases and odors, and to protect the health and safety of all operatives employed therein. Any violation of any of the provisions of this section shall be punishable by a fine of not less than ten dollars nor more than one hundred dollars for each offence.

How offensive trades are to be conducted.

Sec. 4. Any person or persons, owner or owners, occupier or occupiers, having on their premises or the premises occupied by them, any low or marshy place, sink hole or holes, water pond, privy, vault or other nuisance or offensive matter whatever, which is detrimental to or injurious

Owners of marshy places, privy vaults,&c to fill up and abate same on notice from Chief Burgess.

to the health of any citizen or resident of the borough, shall fill up, remove and abate the same upon notice thereof and request so to do by the Chief Burgess or a committee of council charged therewith; and in default thereof within ten days after said notice or request, in writing, the Chief Burgess or council may cause the same to be done and collect the cost thereof together with a penalty not exceeding ten dollars.

SEC. 5. No person or company shall permit or allow any house drainage, waste water from sinks or kitchens, or other liquid refuse to flow into or be cast upon a street or alley, or allow any overflow from any sink or cesspool to escape into any street or alley or into any vacant or unimproved lots, and any person or company violating the provisions of this section shall be guilty of maintaining a nuisance and shall be liable for the expense of the abatement and remedy thereof, and to a penalty not exceeding twenty dollars. *House drainage and liquid refuse not to be thrown into streets, alleys or vacant lots.*

SEC. 6. No waste paper, empty boxes or barrels, or rubbish of any kind shall be thrown or left or placed in any street or alley, and any person violating the provisions of this section, or suffering it to be done or not removing the same upon his, her or their view thereof, when adjacent to or in front of real estate owned or occupied by him or them shall be subject to a fine not exceeding five dollars. *No waste paper or rubbish to be thrown into streets or left there.*

SEC. 7. All snow and ice shall be removed from the pavements and sidewalks, for the entire width of the same, within twenty-four hours after its lodgment, or if any ice cannot be effectually removed then the same shall be covered with ashes, sawdust or similar substance, and every person failing and neglecting to remove or cover the same as herein provided, in front of his or their premises, whether the owner of vacant properties or the occupants of improved premises shall be subject to a penalty of not exceeding five dollars for every sixty feet of frontage so neglected. *Ice and snow to be removed from sidewalks or effectually covered.*

SEC. 8. Any person exposing himself for the purpose of

110

swimming along Front street and the river bank or along the river from the dam to the insection of Front street and Susquehanna Avenue, between hours of six A. M. and nine P. M., shall be subject to a fine of two dollars, and in default of payment thereof shall be committed by the Justice of the Peace before whom the complaint is heard, to the county jail for forty-eight hours.

Swimming along Front street from 6 a. m. to 9 p. m. prohibited.

SEC. 9.—No pig pen shall be built or maintained within the limits of the borough, within forty (40) feet of any well or spring of whter used for drinking purposes, or within forty (40) feet of any street or any inhabited house, or unless constructed in the following manner, viz : So that the floor or floors of the same same shall be not less than eighteen inches from the ground, in order that the filth accumulating under the same may be easily removed ; and such filth accumulating in, about and under the same shall be removed at least once every two weeks, and oftener if so ordered by the Borough Council, and on the failure of any owner or occupier of such premises so to do then the same shall be done by the authority of the said Borough Council, and the expense of removing the same, with twenty per cent. additional, shall be collected from the party so offending, as debts of like amount are collectable by law.

Restrictions on pig pens and how to be constr cted and cleansed.

SEC. 10.—The following named diseases are declared communicable and dangerous to the public's health, viz : Small-pox (variola, varioloid,) cholera (asiatic or epidemic), scarlet fever, (scarlatina, scarlet rash), measles, diptheria, (diptheretic croup, diptheretic sore throat, putrid sore throat), thyphoid fever, yellow fever, spotted fever, (cerebro spinal meningitis) relapsing fever, epidemic dysentery, hydrophobia (rabies) and glanders (farcy).

Diseases dangerous to public health enumerated.

SEC. 11.—Whenever any householder knows that any person in his family or household has a communicable disease, dangerous to the public health, or whenever any physician finds that any person whom he has called upon to visit has a communicable disease dangerous to the public health, he

Householders required to report.

Physicians required to report.

or she shall immediately report the same to the Chief Burgess, giving the street and number or location of the house; on the receipt of which report the said Chief Burgess shall immediately notify the teacher or principal of every school, academy, seminary or kinder garten in the borough requesting said teachers or principals to dispense with the attendance of all pupils residing in the family in which such disease exists, and upon conviction, before any Justice of the Peace, within the borough, for any violation of the provisions of the foregoing section of this ordinance, any householder, physician, Chief Burgess, teacher or principal, as aforesaid, shall be liable to a fine of five dollars.

School teachers to be notified.

Householders, physicians, teachers to be fined for violation.

SEC. 12.—There shall not be a public or church funeral of any person who has died of Asiatic cholera, small-pox, typhus fever, diphtheria, putrid sore throat, yellow fever, scarlet fever or measles, and the family of the deceased shall in all such cases limit the attendance to as few as possible, and take all precautions possible to prevent the exposure of other persons to contagion or infection; and the person authorizing the public notice of death of such person, shall have the name of the disease which caused the death appear in such public notice. Any violation of this ordinance shall be punished by a fine of not less than twenty nor more than one hundred dollars.

Funerals after infectious diseases forbidden

Public notice of cause of death required.

SEC. 13.—Members of any household in which small-pox, diphtheria, putrid sore throat, scarlet fever, Asiatic cholera, yellow fever, typhus fever or measles exists shall abstain from attending places of public amusement, worship or education, and, as far as possible, from visiting private houses. Any violation of this ordinance shall be punished by a fine of five dollars.

Isolation of family required

SEC. 14.—It shall be the duty of the high constable to enforce all provisions of this ordinance as well as the 32, 33, 34, 35, 36 and 37 sections of the borough charter for all the cases therein provided, against all persons violating the same, or any of them, and for this service he shall receive one-half of the fines and penalties upon the offenders. And should

High Constable to enforce this ordinance and provision of charter.

112

Penalty for neglect.

the high constable fail or neglect to proceed against any offender, after notice to him by any citizen of the borough, he shall be subject to a penalty of not exceeding one hundred dollars.

In default of action by High Constable any citizen or other borough officers may inform.

SEC. 15—Provided always, that any citizen or other officer of the borough shall have power, in default of the official action of the said high constable herein provided, to apply to the Chief Burgess or any Justice of the Peace in and for said borough, by information on oath charging any of the offenders in any of the foregoing sections specified and defined, for a writ in nature of a summary process to issue against any person offending against any of the foregoing sections of this ordinance, who shall immediately thereupon issue his writ directing any constable of the said borough, against such offender, commanding him to appear forthwith, as upon a warrant of arrest, to answer such charge or offence; and thereupon the said Chief Burgess or Justice of the Peace shall proceed, without delay, to hear and determine the premises of such charge, and if by him adjudged guilty, each offender shall be at once sentenced to pay the fine or penalty by the provisions of this ordinance defined to be imposed, together with the costs accrued in the premises of such proceeding; but if the magistrate before whom the person so charged shall deem it just to continue the hearing and adjudication of the premises of the charge made as aforesaid, to a time subsequent to the appearance or bringing up of the alleged offender before him, he shall have power to do so, but in that event he shall hold such alleged offender to bail, with sufficient sureties, to appear at such subsequent hearing to answer such charge in a sum adequate to insure such appearance, at which time such magistrate shall proceed to hearing and sentence in manner aforesaid.

Passed Feb. 11, 1887.

G. M. RENN,
Chief Burgess.

AN ORDINANCE

To license and regulate theatrical exhibitions, circuses, concerts, and all other performances and exhibitions.

SECTION 1, Be it enacted and ordained by the Burgesses and Inhabitants of the Borough of Sunbury in town council assembled, and it is enacted and ordained by the authority of the same. That the proprietor or tenant in possession, of every place of amusement and other room or place used for public amusements, shall be required to pay to the Treasurer of the Borough of Sunbury for each and every theatrical or operatic performance or other entertainment, for which an admission fee is charged or where a collection is taken up to pay expenses, given or held or had in such place or room a license fee, which said license shall be as follows: For each performance, by the same person or troupe, not exceeding three, the sum of $2,50 per performance; for not less than three nor more than five successive performances, by the same person or troupe, the sum of $2 00 for each performance; for one weeks performances, by the same person, troupe or company, the sum of ten dollars; Provided, that no license shall be required for any performance given exclusively by residents of the borough for any charitable or other public use and not for personal profit. *(Licenses for theatrical and other entertainments in places of amusement.)*

SECTION 2. Every person or company performing or exhibiting in the open air upon the streets or alleys with any wax figures slight of hand or jugglery or slack or tight rope walking shall pay to the treasurer of said borough a license fee of five dollars for each and every performance. *(Licenses for open air performances.)*

SECTION 3. Every person or company exhibiting upon the public streets for the purpose of selling proprietary medicines or other merchandise shall pay to the treasurer of the borough the sum of two dollars for each and every exhibition or selling aforesaid.

SECTION 4. Every person or company exhibiting in said borough in tents or under canvas shall pay to the Chief Burgess, of the borough a license fee of from ten to twenty- *(Licenses for circuses and other shows under canvas.)*

114

five dollars for each days performances, of the discretion of the Chief Burgess.

Permit and license for street parades of persons exhibiting outside the borough limits.

SEC. 5.—Every company or troupe, exhibiting in tents or under canvas, outside the limits of the borough, but who desire to have a street or out-door exhibition or parade within the limits of the same, shall first obtain a permit from the Chief Burgess and pay a license fee of ten dollars.

Penalty for failure to pay license and how the same shall be recovered.

SEC. 6.—Any person or company or troupe neglecting or refusing to pay the license fee as prescribed in any of the foregoing sections of this ordinance, shall pay, for each such neglect or refusal, a fine equal to double the amount of the license fee as hereinbefore required, to be recovered by summary proceedings to be instituted before the Chief Burgess of the borough or any Justice of the Peace in and for the County of Northumberland, upon information on the oath of the officers charged with the collection thereof, upon whose warrant or summons the goods and chattles as well as the person of the offender may be liable to attachment and seizure forthwith, until payment and satisfaction of the said fine and license fee shall be effected.

Policeman to be employed at cost of proprietor of every place of amusement.

SECTION 7. Every proprietor, manager or tenant in possession of every place of amusement or other room or place used for public purposes shall employ, at his own cost and charge, at least one suitable person, who shall be commissioned by the Chief Burgess as a special police, whose duty it shall be to preserve order in such place during all performances, and it shall be the duty of such officer to make the information and proceed against every person disturbing any such performance or gathering, as provided in the Act of Assembly requiring Justices of the Peace in the County of Northumberland to hear and determine cases of that kind.

Powers and duties thereof.

a.

Passed Feb. 11, 1887.   G. M. RENN. C. B.

a Justices of the peace of this county are impowered by the acts of April 11, 1868, (P. L. 846); 1 May, 1861 (P. L. 682) : 5 April, 1862, (P. L. 273), to hear and determine the following offenses : Blasphemy, disturbance of public meetings, lewdness, cruelty to animals, selling unwholesome provisions or adulterated provisions or medicines, assault and battery, Larceny, (when the value does not exceed $10.) cheating inn-keepers and boarding-house keepers by false pretenses, etc.

AN ORDINANCE.

To regulate the heights, grades, widths, slopes and forms of the streets, gutters, alleys, footwalks and pavements and to provide for the grading, paving and guttering thereof.

SECTION 1. Be it enacted and ordained by the burgesses and inhabitants of the borough of Sunbury in town council assembled, and it is enacted and ordained by the authority of the same. That on Front street, between Shippen and Race streets, the width of the pavement shall be twelve feet and the extent of the porches and steps not more than five feet; on Market street, in the square, the width of the pavement shall be thirteen feet six inches and the extent of the porches and steps shall not be more than five feet nine inches, east and west from the square the *a.*

[margin: Width of pavements and porches or steps fixed]

[margin: Front street.]

[margin: Market street.]

The grades of the curbs at the intersections of the street crossings in the Borough of Sunbury, as adopted by the council Dec. 2nd, 1884 and as far as at that time established, the base being the low water line of the river at that time, a bench mark being the top of the door sill of the office of Ira T. Clement at his planing mill on Race near Third street, which is plus the low water line as thus taken of 18.32 feet, from this base the intersections of streets are then as follows :

Vine and	Third	streets	....not definitily fixed.		
"	"	Fourth	"	....plus	9.0
Race	"	Front	"	.... "	15.0
"	"	Second	"	.... "	17.5
"	"	Third	"	.... "	16.0
"	"	Fourth	"	.... "	9.0
Arch	"	Front	"	.... "	16.5
"	"	Second	"	.... "	18.5
"	"	Third	"	.... "	16.0
"	"	Fourth	"	.... "	12.0
Market	"	Front	"	.... "	15.0
"	"	Square	W	.... "	15.5
"	"	Second	" N	.... "	17.5
"	"	"	" S	.... "	15.5
"	"	Third	" N	.... "	14.0
"	"	"	" S	.... "	13.5
"	"	Square	E	.... "	13.5
"	"	Fourth	"	.... "	12.0
"	"	Fifth	"	.... "	9.0

116

width of the pavement shall be twelve feet and the extent
of the porches shall not be more than five feet; on all other
streets, not less than fifty feet wide, except Second street
from Race to Vine streets, the width of the pavement
shall be ten feet and the extent of the steps and porches
hall not be more than five feet; on all streets forty feet
wide, the width of the pavement shall be eight feet and
the extent of the steps and porches shall not be more than
four feet; on all streets thirty feet wide the width of the
pavement shall be six feet and the extent of porches and
steps shall not be more than three feet; in all alleys,
the width of the pavement (if any shall be laid,) shall not be
more than twenty-four inches. All gutters shall be of trian-
gular slant, and shall be twenty-four inches wide, except on
Market street, where they shall be thirty:

Other streets.

Permanent grades adopted

SECTION 2. The permanent levels, grades and slopes of

Chestnut and Front streets				plus 13.0
"	"	Second	"	" 13.5
"	"	Third	"	" 14.0
"	"	Fourth	"	" 12.0
"	"	Fifth	"	" 9.0
Surface water at Spring Run				minus 5.0
Penn and Front Streets, P. & R. R. R				plus 19.3
"	"	Second	" "	" 15.6
"	"	Third	" "	" 13.2
"	"	Fourth	" "	" 13.2
Walnut and Front streets				" 13.0
"	"	Second	"	" 13.75
"	"	Third	"	" 14.5
"	"	Fourth	"	" 14.0
Spruce	"	Front	"	" 12.0
"	"	Second	"	" 15.0
"	"	Third	"	" 14.0
"	"	Fourth	"	" 14.6

The following cross-sections were made May 14th, 1885, and confirmed by
Council :

Pine and Front streets				plus 12.0
"	"	Second	"	" 13.5
"	"	Third	"	" 14.0
Lombard and Front		"		" 12.0
"	"	Second	"	" 13.5

117

the several streets and alleys shall be as heretofore fixed by the council in accordance with the profiles and recommenda- of the borough regulators, which said grades, slopes and levels are hereby adopted, ratified and confirmed and it is directed that the same be printed in the ordinance book,now being prepared under the direction of the council, as a note to this section. All pavements, gutters and streets shall conform to the grades and levels as fixed thereby ; Provided that where permanent levels and grades have not been here- tofore established, the same shall be established whenever occasion may require, and thereupon the streets, pavements and gutters shall conform therewith. All pavements to conform thereto

Section 3. All the streets of the borough shall be curbed, sidewalks paved and the streets guttered by the owners of lots of ground respectively fronting on said streets, in conformity with these regulations and the grades so Streets to be gut- tered and pave- ments laid by lot owners.

South and Front streets .... plus 12.0
"   " Second   "   .... " 13.5
Bainbridge and Front "   .... " 12.0
"   " Second "   .... " 13.5
The following cross-sections in the upper part of Borough were made June 15th, 1885, and confirmed by Council :
Line and Front streets, bank................................. plus 16.1
" " Susquehanna Ave .... " 10.5
" " Rail Road   "   .... " 9.5
" " Second streets.................................. " 8.5
Masser and Front " bank................................ " 15.5
" " Susquehanna Ave................... " 11.5
" " Rail Road Ave.......................... " 10.5
Grreenough and Front streets, bank.................. " 13.5
"   " Fort Augusta Ave.................. " 13.0
"   " Susquehanna " .... " 12.5
"   " Rail Road   "   .... " 11.5
Packer   " Front streets.............................. " 13.5
"   " Fort Augusta Ave............. " 14.0
"   " Susquehanna " .... " 14.5
"   " Rail Road " .... " 15.5
Amy   " Susquehanna " .... " 14.5
"   " Rail Road   "   .... " 15.5
Alice   " Front streets.......................... " 13.5
"   " Fort Augusta Ave................... " 14.0

118

established, and all such curbing and paving is required to be done in a good and workmanlike manner of good and substantial stone or brick, under the superintendence of the borough regulators; Provided that the owners of vacant or unimproved lots may lay temporary sidewalks of plank or other suitable material, to be at least three feet in width, such temporary walks to be replaced by a brick or stone pavement immediately upon the improvement of such premises; and provided that in case of improved lots, where there is no building, there the pavement shall be of the width of five feet measured from the outside line of the pavement inwards, which pavement shall be brought to the full width whenever there are buildings erected on the excepted part.

Temporary sidewalks may be laid in front of vacant lots, to be replaced when improved.

SECTION 4. That wherever there are no pavements, or where the pavements already laid so differ from the established grade and the other adjacent pavements as to render the same dangerous to life or limb, it shall be the duty of the Chief Burgess, and he is hereby required, upon the petition of five or more residents of the borough, verified by affidavit, showing the facts and that they labor under great inconvenience by reason thereof, to issue a precept to the owners and occupiers of lots, fronting on the streets named in the said petition, directing and requiring that the pavements be laid or relaid, as the case may be, within sixty days after such notice, of the widths and materials and in the manner herein provided; and upon the failure of any owner or occupier, of any lot of ground so notified, to cause the curbing and paving of the side walks to be made and done as aforesaid, within the time prescribed in said notice, that then the Chief Burgess is hereby authorized, directed, empowered and required to cause said pavement, side or

Where there are no pavements, and where pavements differ from grade, citizens may petition Chief Burgess.

Chief Burgess to issue precept to owner and occupier to lay same, and in default to cause same to be laid, and collect cost thereof.

Alice street and Susquehanna ave		plus 14.5
"	" Rail Road "	" 15.5
Julia	" Front streets	" 13.5
"	" Fort Augusta Ave	" 14.0
"	" Susquehanna "	" 14.5
"	" Rail Road "	" 15.5

foot walks, paving and curbing to be made and done in accordance with the act of assembly in such case made and provided and under the direction and control of the borough regulators, and the Chief Burgess is hereby directed and required to collect the cost of the work and material required, with twenty per cent advance thereon from the owner or owners into the manner directed by the provisions of the Act of Assembly in such case made and provided.

Passed Feb. 11, 1887.

G. M. RENN,
Chief Burgess.

NOTE.—All appropriation ordinances are omitted, and the general form is inserted as an appendix.

BY-LAWS AND RULES OF ORDER

Adopted by the Town Council of the Borough of Sunbury, July 10, 1855.

Chief Burgess to preside at all meetings of council, and perform all duties enjoined on him

SECTION 1. The Chief Burgess shall preside over all meetings of the Council and perform generally all such duties as are enjoined on him by the Act of Incorporation, by-laws, ordinances and resolutions of the Council, and in **Second Burgess to act in his absence or inability,** case of his absence or other inability to act, the Second Burgess shall act, and in case of his absence the Council **Of president *pro tem*.** may from time to time elect a President *pro tem.*, as occasion may require, who shall exercise the same authority and perform the same duties that are or may be enjoined on the Chief Burgess.

SEC. 2. The chair will decide all questions of order arising during the deliberations of the board, but any member deeming himself aggrieved by the decision of the chair **Of appeals from decisions of the chair.** may take an appeal to the board of Council, which appeal, if seconded, shall be put to the board by the chair and be decided by them without debate.

Committees appointed by him.

SEC. 3.—The chair will appoint all committees unless the board of Council shall by resolution determine otherwise.

Stated meetings to be held monthly.

SEC. 4.—The board of Council shall meet statedly for the transaction of business on the first Tuesday evening in each **Time of** month, at the following hours, viz: In January, February, October, November and December at 7 o'clock P. M.; March, April and September at 7½ o'clock P. M.; in May, June, July and August at 8 o'clock P. M. Adjourned **Adjourned and special meetings** and special meetings may be held from time to time as they shall be deemed necessary, Provided that all adjourned meetings held in any month shall be considered as a continuance of the first or stated meeting of such month.

Members not to leave room without permission.

SEC. 5.—No member will be at liberty to leave the Council room after roll call without permission first obtained from the chair.

SEC. 6.—Seven members shall constitute a quorum for the transaction of business. *Quorum.*

The following order of business shall be observed at all meetings of the board : *Order of business.*

1st. The roll of members will be called by the Town Clerk, or in his absence by a member of the Council appointed by the board to discharge that duty, and the absentees duly noted. *Roll call.*

SEC. 7.—Minutes shall be read ; if objected to in whole or in part, the objection shall be heard and correction made, if required, so as to make them consistent with the facts ; if not objected to they shall stand approved, without a vote, and be recorded thus approved in a book provided for that purpose. *Reading and correction of minutes.*

NOTE.—After the minutes are read the chair will proclaim thus : "Gentlemen, you have heard the minutes read, if there are no objections they will stand approved ;" if there are no objections he will add. "Mr. Clerk, the minutes stand approved." *Form of question on approval*

SEC. 8.—Committees will report, through their chairman, in the order of precedence in which they were appointed. Reports of committees must in all cases be in writing. Reports of committes will be acted upon by the board as is usual in other deliberative bodies. Minority reports may be heard at the discretion of the Council. *Reports of committees to be in writing and made by chairman.* *Minority reports.*

SEC. 9.—Memorials and communications to Council will be presented and such action taken thereon as may seem expedient to Council : Provided, That the rules which govern deliberative bodies must in all cases be complied with. And provided further, That action shall be taken upon no memorial, petition or communication which is not in writing, and clothed in respectful language. *Memorials and petitions.*

SEC. 10.—Individual business will be attended to, viz : Reception and action upon accounts, claims, &c. *Individual business, accounts, &c.*

SEC. 11.—Such new business as deemed necessary and expedient, suggested by members of Council and not otherwise provided for by these rules. *New business.*

Of business at special meetings.

SEC. 12.—At special meetings the business for which Council was specially convened shall be first acted upon, and no new matter shall receive the attention of Council till such special matter is disposed of.

Resolutions and motions to be in writing.

SEC. 13.—All resolutions or motions shall be submitted in writing, and shall be seconded before received.

Members to rise to address chair

SEC. 14.—When addressing the chair members shall rise from their seats; a member to whom the floor is awarded shall not be interrupted, (except by a call to order,) while speaking. Members shall not speak at any one time for a greater period than twenty minutes.

Speeches limited to 20 minutes

Form of presenting paper to council.

SEC. 15.—A member wishing to present a paper must state its general import, and before it is read the chair shall take the voice of the Council thus: "Shall the paper held by the gentleman be read? If there be no objection it will be read; let the paper be read." If there is objection the ayes and nays shall be taken without debate.

All reports and petitions to be laid on table unless otherwise ordered.

SEC. 16.—At the first reading of any memorial, petition, report of committee, remonstrance, ordinance, or other paper, (excepting always simple resolutions) upon motion, it shall be laid upon the table, unless particularly directed by the board, by a motion, regularly made, put, and carried.

Two-thirds vote requisite to pass an ordinance at first meeting.

SEC. 17.—No ordinance shall be passed into a law, at the same sitting at which it is introduced, unless concurred in by two-thirds of the members present.

Committee of whole.

SEC. 18.—Upon motion made and carried the Council may resolve itself into a committee of the whole when the Chief Burgess, having first appointed a member to the chair, may participate in the deliberations, as other members of the board.

Duties of chairman of committees; committee may appoint their own.

SEC. 19.—The person first named on a committee will be chairman of that committee and shall have power to convene the committee for the discharge of its duties, Provided, That all committees after being convened may appoint their own chairman.

Duties of Town Clerk.

SEC. 20.—It shall be the duty of the Town Clerk to duly notify all chairmen of committees of their appointment;

123

and he shall cause members of Council to be served with notices of special meetings at least one day previous thereto. He shall further be required to surrender the books, papers and records in his possession to his successor in office in good order and condition, and for neglecting or refusing to so surrender them, having been duly notified, he shall forfeit and pay the sum of twenty-five dollars, to be recoverable as debt of like amounts are by law recoverable, and paid into the treasury for the use of the borough.

SEC. 21.—Members of Council shall be subjected to the following fines and penalties, viz : Penalties.

Absence at stated meetings, ... $1.00
Absence at roll call, ... .05
Leaving the room without permission,...... .25
Refusing to obey a call to order,........... 1.00

The Town Clerk shall be fined for neglecting to serve notices, five cents for each notice.

Reasonable excuses will in cases be accepted.

APPENDIX.

GENERAL FORM FOR APPROPRIATION ORDINANCE.

AN ORDINANCE

To provide for the ordinary expenses of the Borough and the interest on the funded debt for the year ending March ......

SECTION 1.—Be it ordained by the Burgesses and inhab itants of the Borough of Sunbury in town council assembled, that the following sums shall be and the same are hereby appropriated and set apart for the purposes specified, for and during the fiscal year ending March........

1st.—For the payment of interest on the borough debt the sum of.............................dollars, or so much thereof as may be necessary.

2nd.—For the payment of the annual installment to be set apart for the redemption of the outstanding bonds, loan of 1881, the sum of......................dollars.

3d.—For the payment of the State tax on the bonded debt the sum of......................dollars.

4th.—For the support and maintenance of the fire department and ordinary and incidental repairs to apparatus, to be divided among the companies as the Council may direct, the sum of.................... .....dollars, or so much thereof as may be necessary.

5th.—For the salaries of the Borough officers and the Overseers of the Poor the sum of.......... .
dollars, or so much thereof as may be necessary.

6th.—For the payment of the High Constable the sum of...................... dollars, or so much thereof as may be necessary.

7th.—For the ordinary and incidental expenses the sum of ... . dollars, or so much thereof as may be necessary.

8th.—For the maintenance and repairs of streets, alleys, river bank and Spring Run the sum of .. . . .. dollars, or so much thereof as may be necessary.

9th.—For the lighting of the streets and the purchase of new posts the sum of. ... .dollars, or so much thereof as may be adjudged due upon a contract for that purpose, to be paid monthly.

10th.—For the repairs and care of the graveyard, including pay the workmen, the sum of ... ... dollars, or so much thereof as may be necessary.

11th.—For the payment of the rental due the Sunbury Water Company for the use of water plugs the sum of.... ... .dollars, payable quarterly, as specified in the contract.

12th.—For the relief of the poor, the expenses of the poor house, the support of the inmates and the pay of the necessary employees, the sum of........... .... dollars, not to include any compensation to any Overseer of the Poor.

13th.—For the support of the insane poor chargeable to the Borough the sum of . ...dollars, or so much thereof as may be necessary.

INDEX.

(Note. All references are to the pages.)

128

BOROUGH (CONTINUED.)

Corporate powers, 3.
To maintain a ferry and ferrymen, 4.
To have exclusive ferry right, 4.
Powers and privileges of, and restrictions 5
May build embankment on lands of Thomas Grant 28.
Limits extended, 29.
Repeal of act extending limits, 34.
Divided into east and west wards, 36.
Limits extended by repeal of act on page 34, 39.
Borough cannot be a stockholder in any corporation, 46.
To pay for private pro,erty taken for public use, 47.
Court may change limits of 51.
Adjacent lands may be annexed to, 51.
May license theatres and other amusements, 52.
Division of, into five wards and decree of court, 70.

BOROUGH OFFICERS. (GENERALLY.)

What to be elected, 1
To be qualified, 5.
Penalty for refusing to act, 7.
What are to give bond, 31.
Salaries to be fixed by council, 32.
Term and salary of, not to be increased after election. 45.
How school directors and councilmen to be elected, 49.
What to be elected in the several wards, and in borough, 50.
How certain vacancies are to be filled, 61.
When terms of office are to begin, 63.
What are to be elected since five wards erected, 71.

ASSESSORS.

To be elected, 11.
To aid in levying road tax (obsolete,) 12.
To be elected in each ward and duties of, 50, 71.

AUDITORS.

To be appointed by council, 32.
Salary to be fixed by council, 32.
Duties of, 16, 17, 33.
To be elected by voters, where divided into wards, 50, 71.
When to meet, 63.

129

BOROUGH OFFICERS—(Continued.)

Auditor.

To publish annual statements of receipts and expenses, 63.
Penalty for neglect of duty, 64.
To cancel coupons upon settling Treasurer's accounts, 96.
To form part of committee to invest sinking fund, 96.

Burgesses.

And assistants to be elected, 1.
To summon town meetings for passage of ordinances, 7.
To appoint regulators or surveyors, 8.
To allow taxes before collection, 13.
To fill vacancies in office of supervisor, 13.
To audit accounts, 16.
Jurisdiction as to fines and forfeitures, 10–24.
Form part of town council, 26.
Second to be elected, 35.
Assistant to be elected, 71.

Chief Burgess.

To be commissioned by Governor, 2.
Forms a part of the town council, 26.
Authorized to sell river bank for wharves (doubtful,) 27.
To issue warrant for collection of taxes, 31, 65.
To sign all orders for the payment of money, 32.
Salary to be fixed by council, 32.
To be elected by the qualified voters, 35, 71.
To enforce by-laws and rules of order, 35.
To receive fines imposed for disorderly conduct, 77.
To proceed on his own view against drunken and disorderly persons, 83.
Not to suffer any appropriation to be overdrawn, 92.
Duty of as to sinking fund, 96.
Duty of as to communicable diseases, 110.
To license shows under canvas, 114.
To license street parades of shows, 114.
To commission policemen for places of amusement, 114.
To issue precepts for laying pavements, 118.
Where pavements are not laid to cause same to be done, 118.
To preside at all meetings of council, 120.
To appoint all committees, 120.

BOROUGH OFFICERS—(Continued.)

Councilmen.

Eight to be elected in borough, 26.
To form a part of the town council, 26.
Divided between east and west wards, 36.
To be elected in all wards, 50.
Election and term of office of, regulated, 62.
How vacancies in office of to be filled, 62.
Two to be elected in each ward, 71.

Council. (See also Burgesses.)

Powers of and who constitute, 26–27.
Ordinances adopted by may be revoked at town meeting, 27.
Powers of enlarged, 29.
To regulate pavements, streets and gutters, 30.
To compel curbing, paving and guttering, 30,
To make regulations about fires and to purchase apparatus, 30.
May make appropriations to fire companies, 30.
To levy taxes for borough purposes, 30.
To elect treasurer and collector, 31.
To constitute a board of appeal, 31.
To pass all bills, 31.
To fix all salaries and commissions, 32.
To appoint auditors, 32.
To establish night watch and special police, 33.
May change the names of the streets, 33.
To levy and collect road and poor taxes, 33.
To fill vacancies in offices of town clerk and high constable, 35.
To construct a bank along Front street, 37.
Action of in donating money to erection of court house legalized, 36.
May levy ten mills each for borough, road and poor purposes, 38.
May borrow money and issue bonds, 38.
Duty of council in extension of Second and Fourth streets, 40.
Authorized to build or provide a lock up, 42.
To make regulations for markets and market days, 44.
To regulate hawking, peddling, and weights and measures, 44.
Authorized to borrow $35,000, 44.
Must vote viva voce in electing officers, &c., 46.
Street railway cannot be built without consent of, 47.
To license theatres and shows, &c., 53.
To regulate erection of wooden buildings, 54.
To publish financial statement, 58.
To provide for all expenditures by appropriation, 92.

BOROUGH OFFICERS—(Continued.)

Council.

Not to expend any money without an appropriation, 92.
·Consent of majority of whole required to appropriate money, 92.
To grant no order except on written vouchers, 93.
To maintain inviolate the sinking fund, 95.
To approve bonds of overseers of the poor, 98.
To regulate conduction of offensive trades, 108.

High Constable.

To be elected, 2.
To summon town meetings, 7.
To give bonds, 31.
Salary to be fixed by the council, 32.
Council to fill vacancies in the office of, 35.
To collect fines for violation of by-laws, 35.
To impound and sell cattle running at large, 75, 76, 78.
To arrest boys and others disorderly on the streets, 77.
To enforce health and nuisance ordinances and charter, 111.

Market Clerk—(See Markets.)

Overseers of the Poor.

Two to be elected, 32.
To sign all orders for the relief of paupers, 32.
Salary to be fixed by council, 32.
Election and term of office of, 62.
To be required to give bonds, 68.
To make and submit to council estimates of expenses, 93.
To expend money appropriated and report monthly, 93.
To give bonds in $5,000 before entering on duties, 98.

Regulators or Surveyors.

To be appointed and duties of, 8.
To determine party walls and street lines, 8.
To regulate streets, sidewalks, gutters, 8.
Persons aggrieved by decisions of may appeal to court, 10.
To regulate partition fences, 10.
May direct removal of obstructions from streets, 19–20.

BOROUGH OFFICERS -(Continued.)

Town Clerk.

To call roll at all meetings of council, 121.
To issue notices for all meetings of council, 122.

Treasurer.

To be elected by council, 31.
To give bonds as required by council, 31.
To proceed against collector in case of default, 31.
Salary to be fixed by council, 32.
To receive fines for locomotives exceeding maximum speed, 80.
To receive fines for selling or discharging fireworks, 81.
Officers, &c., to settle accounts with before end of official year, 93.
Duties of as to bonds and coupons, 94.
To pay no orders drawn by overseers until security given, 99.
To receive licenses for performances in all places of amusement or on
public streets, 113.

BUILDINGS.

Council may prohibit erection of wooden, 54.
To be provided with sufficient means of ingress and egress, 107.
To be ventilated and drained, 107.

BY-LAWS AND RULES OF ORDER.

Chief Burgess authorized to enforce, 35.

(See Rules of Order.)

CEMETERIES.

Regulation of vested in court, 67.
Sexton to be elected by council, 77.
Duties and compensation of, 77.

CATTLE.

Running at large of certain kinds prohibited, 75, 76, 78.

CHIEF BURGESS—(See Borough Officers.)

184

FERRIES—(Continued.)

Exclusive right of in borough, 4.
Penalty for infringement, 4.
Right of in Scott and Hunter farms to remain, 29.

FINES, FORFEITURES AND PENALTIES.

For encroaching by buildings on streets or alleys, 8.
Building without procuring lines from regulators, 9.
Casting dirt and rubbish from improvements into streets, 19.
Casting ashes or any filth or rubbish upon streets, 19.
Dumping rubbish out of wagons into streets without consent, 20.
Running foul liquors into streets or alleys, 20.
Butchers keeping putrid matter or filth at slaughter house, 20.
Leaving carrion or filth on streets or vacant lots, 20.
Obstructing sewers, 21.
Making pavements contrary to regulations, 21.
Encroachments by porches, steps or bay-windows, 22.
Injuring or displacing drainage or other water pipes, 23.
How recoverable for breach of charter regulations, 24.
Keeping more than twenty-five pounds of gunpowder in house, 24.
Fast riding and driving, 74.
Letting horse, sheep, swine or geese run at large, 75.
Letting colts run at large, 76.
Congregating on streets to make noise or commit nuisance, 77.
Driving on Market Square, 78.
Letting mules and goats run at large, 78.
Locomotives exceeding speed of five miles per hour, 80.
Selling or discharging fireworks, 81.
Drunkenness and disorderly conduct, 82.
Violations of market ordinance, 87.
Blocking streets and sidewalks by standing or gathering, 98.
Creating, maintaining or contributing to any nuisance, 107.
Throwing refuse or garbage into streets, lot or "Gut," 108.
Keeping putrid or decaying matter on premises, 108.
Conducting offensive trades without permit, 108.
Having any pond, privy or other nuisance injurious to health, 108.
Running house drainage and liquid refuse into streets or lot, 109.
Leaving waste paper, boxes or barrels on streets or alleys, 109.
Failure to remove ice or snow, or cover same, 109.
Exposing person for swimming from 6 A. M. to 9 P. M., 109.
Violating regulations about pigpens, 110.
Failure to report communicable diseases, 110.
Teachers permitting persons exposed to, to attend school, 111.

FINES, FORFEITURES AND PENALTIES— (CONTINUED.)

(On officers, see BOROUGH OFFICER S.)

FIRES.

FIRE WORKS.

FUNERALS.

GEESE.

GOATS.

GRADES AND LEVELS.

GUNPOWDER.

PARKS.

Market Square not to be driven upon, 78.
River bank set apart as, 100.

PARTY WALLS. (See REGULATORS under BOROUGH OFFICERS.)

PAVEMENTS.

Ashes and other filth not to be cast on, 19.
Penalty for making contrary to directions of regulators, 21.
To be regulated by the council, 30.
Penalty on persons blocking, 98.
Width of on Second street north of Race, 101.
Snow and ice to be removed from or covered, 109.
General ordinance regulating width of, 115.
Permanent grades and levels for established, 116.
Maximum projection of porches and steps on, 116.
All pavements to conform thereto, 117.
To be laid and gutters made by lot owners, 117.
Temporary may be laid in front of vacant lots, 118.
Where needed or unsafe citizens to petition chief burgess, 118.
Proceedings to compel laying or relaying of, 118.

PIG PENS.

Forbidden within forty feet of any house or well, 110.
Manner in which they are to be constructed, 110.

POLICE.

Special and night watch may be established by council, 33.
To be appointed for all places of amusement, 114.
To enforce acts of assembly regarding disturbances of, 114.

PORCHES AND STEPS.

Not to project upon Second street north of Race street, 101.
Maximum projection of all others fixed, 116.

(See FINES, &c.)

PUBLIC MEETINGS.

Order to be preserved in all places of, 114.
Persons disturbing to be proceeded against, 114.

TOWN CLERK. (See Borough Officers.)

TOWN MEETINGS. (See Burgesses and Council under Borough Officers.)

WARDS.

> Borough divided into east and west, and their boundaries, 36.
> Each to form a separate election district, 36.
> Boundaries re-defined, 39.
> How new ones to be erected and all proceedings thereon, 47.
> Proceedings on division of this borough into five wards, 70.
> Officers to be elected in each of them, 71.

WOODEN BUILDINGS.

> Council may prohibit erection of, 54.